MILITARY AIRCRAFT BONEYARDS

NICHOLAS A. VERONICO,
A. KEVIN GRANTHAM,
AND SCOTT THOMPSON

MBI Publishing Company

THIS BOOK IS DEDICATED TO TILLIE AND WILLIAM T. LARKINS FOR THEIR EFFORTS TO RECORD AVIATION HISTORY IN PRINT AND ON FILM, AND FOR THEIR GENEROSITY IN SHARING THAT COLLECTION WITH OTHERS.

First published in 2000 by MBI Publishing Company, 729 Prospect Avenue, PO Box 1, Osceola, WI 54020-0001 USA

© Nicholas A. Veronico, 2000

MBI Publishing Company books are also available at discounts in bulk quantity for industrial or sales-promotional use. For details write to Special Sales Manager at Motorbooks International Wholesalers & Distributors, 729 Prospect Avenue, PO Box 1, Osceola, WI 54020-0001 USA.

Library of Congress Cataloging-in-Publication Data

Veronico, Nicholas A.
    Military aircraft boneyards/Nicholas A. Veronico, A. Kevin Grantham & Scott Thompson.
        p. cm.
    Includes bibliographical references and index.
    ISBN 0-7603-0820-9 (pbk. : alk. paper)
        1. Airplanes, Military—United States. 2. Surplus military property, American—History—20th century. 3. Reconstruction Finance Corporation. Office of Surplus property—History.
    I. Grantham, A. Kevin. II. Thompson, Scott.
    III. Title.

UG1243.V47   2000
358.4'162137—dc21   00-041866

front cover
A stack of obsolete Republic F-84s awaits the smelter circa 1959. These straight wing, subsonic jets were being replaced by the Century-Series supersonic interceptors. *Pima Air and Space Museum*

frontispiece
A cannibalized B-52 stands as testament to the policy of reusing as much of an aircraft as possible before disposal. This aircraft was once an important vertebrae in the backbone of America's nuclear arsenal. *Nicholas A. Veronico*

title page
A sea of tall tail B-52Ds—nearly 100 visible—were reduced to ingots shortly after this July 1993 photo was taken. *Nicholas A. Veronico*

back cover, top
B-52s are cut into five sections to comply with the Strategic Arms Reduction Treaty (START). After elimination as a flyable aircraft, the carcasses are left for 90 days to allow Russian satellites and inspectors to verify the bomber's destruction. *Jerry Fugere*

back cover, bottom
It is very unusual to see nose art on a Carpetbagger aircraft, especially a yellow and black striped winged tiger. This engineless B-24 has a ferry tank installed in the left front bomb bay. Note that the P-38s behind the B-24 still have their engines as if awaiting potential buyers. *Robert A. Kropp Collection*

Edited by Michael Haenggi
Designed by Doug Tiedman

Printed in China

CONTENTS

ACKNOWLEDGMENTS

The arsenal of democracy produced a tremendous number of airplanes during World War II and into the early 1950s. So many, in fact, that military and ex-military planes were commonplace. In the late 1940s and early 1950s, every airport and duster strip had a surplus fighter or bomber sitting in the weeds. With so many planes around, only die-hard aviation enthusiasts exposed high-priced film on "junk" aircraft. Thus, photos of aircraft in storage before 1960 are difficult to come by. The authors hope that readers will take a moment to acknowledge many of the names in the photo credits to recognize who was shooting in the early days. In addition, the names of those who provided assistance to the project, including photographs, follow below. All are owed a debt of gratitude for their patience and generosity in assisting with this project.

The authors are indebted to, and were motivated by the work of, William T. Larkins. His unique photos of Kingman and Cal-Aero Fields stirred the imagination of many an aviation enthusiast. Larkins' research formed the starting point and motivation for this work. His generosity, trust, and guidance have enabled the authors to provide the first book-length discussion of surplus aircraft from the massive scrapping operations that occurred after World War II to today's aircraft recycling program at the Aerospace Maintenance And Regeneration Center (AMARC).

Many people provided access to their personal or professional collections, or granted the authors interviews. Their assistance is greatly appreciated and include the following: Ian Abbott; Richard Allnutt; Holly Amundson; Betty Anderson; Brian Baker; Caroline and Ray Bingham; Claire and Joe Bradshaw; Darlene and Roger Cain; Cindy Coan–Pima Air and Space Museum; Dan Collier; Harry M. Davidson; Ed Davies; John Dienst; Robert F. Dorr; Jill Dunbar; Jim Dunn; James H. Farmer; Jerry Fugere; Harry Gann; Scott E. Germain; Wayne McPherson Gomes; Jackie Grantham; K. B. Haack; Todd Hackbarth; Michael Haenggi; Dan Hagedorn; Ervan Hare; Woody Harris; Ed Harrow–Pima Air and Space Museum; Ted Holgerson; Earl Holmquist; the late Clay Jansson; Norm Jukes; Phil Kortas; Robert A. Kropp; Gerald Liang; Michael Lombardi–Boeing Historical Archives; Tom Lubbesmeyer–Boeing Historical Archives; Thomas Wm. McGarry; Yvonne and Dale Messimer; Ken Miller; Stephanie Mitchell–Pima Air and Space Museum; Julian Myers; Fred Nimz; Bill North; Dan O'Hara; Dave Ostrowski; Milo Peltzer; Taigh Ramey; Bernard Schulte; Doug Scroggins; Mel Shettle; Ron Strong; Kirsten Tedesco–Pima Air and Space Museum; Linda Terrin–Mohave County Historical Society; Norman P. Thompson; Lisa, Adam, Lucas, and Nathan Thompson; Terry Vanden-Heuvel–AMARC; Karen and Armand H. Veronico; Kathleen and Tony Veronico; Terry Waddington; Randy Walker; Tim Weinschenker; G. W. Wilson; Lindsey S. Youngblood; and the staffs of the Kirtland AFB Historian's Office (Albuquerque, N.M.), Museum of the Western Prairie (Altus, Okla.), Pima Air and Space Museum (Tucson, Ariz.), and the Stillwater Airport Memorial Museum (Stillwater, Okla.).

—*Nicholas A. Veronico*
San Carlos, California
—*A. Kevin Grantham*
Frederick, Maryland
—*Scott A. Thompson*
Elk Grove, California

CHAPTER 1
The Process of Aircraft Disposal After World War II

Mention the name *Kingman* to anyone even casually versed in aviation lore and the image of thousands of aluminum veterans lined up in neat rows awaiting the scrapper's blade comes to mind. And, indeed, Kingman, Arizona, was the final destination for more than 5,400 surplus bombers and fighters at the end of World War II. However, Kingman was only one of five major airplane scrapping operations undertaken in late 1946 and early 1947 to liquidate excess American World War II military airplanes. Furthermore, what happened at Kingman and the other scrapyards across the southern United States was just the highly visible epilogue of a deliberate, carefully crafted policy of aircraft disposal.

In today's world, where a pristine P-38 Lightning commands a seven-figure price tag that sends expeditions to Greenland to dig airframes out from below hundreds of feet of ice, it may be difficult to understand why the American aerial armada was so effectively salvaged and smelted after World War II. Today's warbird enthusiast often speaks in outrage at a government and policy that destroyed our historic airplanes in such a wanton fashion. But a step back to look at the very real problem of how to deal with tens of thousands of virtually worthless airplanes, not to mention all of the other accumulated surpluses from the war effort, provides a perspective missing from modern view.

The policymakers in the United States government, both civil and military, realized very early in the war the problems of demobilization and disposal of the planned fleet of war planes—not yet rolling off production lines. Studies began in 1943 that examined earlier efforts and the potential impact of war surpluses on the postwar world. Policy was established in 1944 that reflected the results of these studies and set the course for dealing with the coming aircraft surplus.

Although occasionally plagued by perceived mismanagement and vocal critics, the government largely pursued its established policy and by 1948 had completed its initial round of World War II aircraft disposal. Any modern sentimental hindsight that focuses on the undignified destruction of massed American warplanes might be accurate only to fault the U.S. government for being, perhaps, unusually efficient in the prosecution of its aircraft disposal policy.

Navy and Marine Corps F-4 Phantom IIs await a Tucson rainstorm, January 14, 2000. Tail markings range from Navy VF-154 to Marine Corps VMFA-314. *Nicholas A. Veronico*

In spite of the massive scrapping operations after World War I, as seen here at Romorantin, France, huge amounts of surplus aircraft had a negative impact on America's aviation industry during the 1920s and 1930s. The Surplus War Property Administration (SWPA) was set up during World War II to prevent the aviation industry from collapsing at the end of the war. *Armand H. Veronico Collection*

U.S. Navy Lockheed P-3 Orions in storage during May 1996. Some of these aircraft have been supplied to allied nations through foreign military sales. Recipient countries include Greece, Thailand, Chile, and Australia. *Nicholas A. Veronico*

The Task at Hand: An Overview

American manufacturers produced approximately 294,000 aircraft between June 1940 and August 1945, most of which were delivered to the U.S. government for military use. Of those built, about 70 percent, or 205,000, were combat aircraft, the remainder being trainers and transports.[1] The inventory held by U.S. military forces in July 1945 approximated 106,707 aircraft. Of these, the Army Air Forces (AAF) held 65,795, with the U.S. Navy (USN) and Marine Corps (USMC) claiming another 40,912 aircraft.[2] This was deemed to be far in excess of any postwar military requirement.

In addition, the military services had already declared more than 30,000 aircraft, mostly trainers, as surplus.[3] Combined with pending Lend-Lease returns from overseas and excess aircraft production, the potential pool of surplus aircraft numbered at least 150,000.

As part of the demobilization process, policy established that the AAF and USN would internally evaluate aircraft needs and release excess aircraft for disposal. Those aircraft based domestically were transferred to the Reconstruction Finance Corporation (RFC), a government corporation assigned the aircraft disposal task. In November 1945, estimates projected that a total of 117,210 aircraft would eventually be transferred as surplus, of which 89,180 would be combat types with the balance transport and light aircraft.[4]

The AAF, after evaluating its postwar requirements, retained a large number of aircraft in AAF-controlled storage depots for future use. As of May 1, 1946, the AAF was storing 15,050 aircraft, primarily B-17s, B-25s, B-29s, A-26s, C-47s, P-47s, and P-51s, at eight depots.[5] Major depots were established at South Plains Army Air Field (Lubbock), TX; Patterson Army Air Field (Dayton), OH; Garden City, KS; and Davis-Monthan Army Air Field (Tucson), AZ

The USN also retained a substantial inventory of aircraft for future use, with the majority being stored at Naval Air Station in Jacksonville, Florida, and Naval Air Field in Litchfield Park, Arizona. By 1947 over 1,000 aircraft of 12 different types were in storage at Litchfield Park.[6]

Those domestic aircraft deemed surplus to military requirements, primarily due to mission, obsolescence, or combat usage, were transferred to the RFC. The first large flood of transfers began in mid-1945 when nearly 30,000 training aircraft were released from the military.[7] With the end of hostilities in August 1945, combat aircraft, particularly war-wearies, were quickly evaluated as unneeded and transferred to the RFC at a rate of 175 aircraft per day. In 1945 a total of 21,600 combat aircraft were released to the RFC, with more than half the transfers occurring after October 1945.[8]

The RFC established at least 60 aircraft depots around the country to store or sell surplus aircraft in accordance with the government's disposal policy.

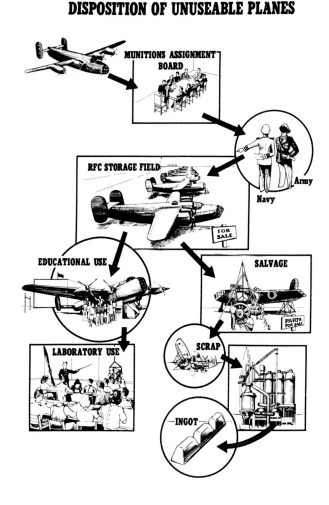

DISPOSITION OF UNUSEABLE PLANES

The RFC issued this diagram to educate the public on how it planned to dispose of the vast fleet of World War II aircraft. *Grantham Collection*

Single-Engine
PRIMARY TRAINER AIRPLANES
$875 TO $2400

Through Reconstruction Finance Corporation
Government Surplus Property

These planes can be used for flight instruction, personal transportation, crop dusting, ranch or forest patrol and other purposes. Types available are Fairchild Army models PT-19, PT-23; Boeing Army models PT-17, PT-27; Navy models N2S-1, N2S-3, N2S-4; Ryan PT-22; and Naval Aircraft Factory N3N-3.

They are powered with in-line or radial type engines ranging from 160 to 235 horsepower, and are two-place, tandem, open cockpit monoplanes or biplanes of composite construction. These models are type-certificated but individual planes must be repaired to meet Civil Aeronautics Administration airworthiness requirements for civilian flight.

All of the above types formerly were used by the Army and Navy in their respective pilot training programs.

Information on sales procedure, location of available aircraft, and selling prices may be obtained from your nearest Sales Center.

SALES CENTERS
(Cities listed alphabetically by States)

LOCATION	AIRPORT
Birmingham, Alabama	Municipal
Phoenix, Arizona	Thunderbird II
Tueson, Arizona	Ryan
Wickenburg, Arizona	Echeverria
Pine Bluff, Arkansas	Grider
West Helena, Arkansas	Thompson-Robbins
Blythe, California	Gary
Concord, California	Sherman
Fresno, California	Chandler Field
Hemet, California	Ryan
Ontario, California	Cal-Aero
Denver, Colorado	Rutledge
Miami, Florida	Chapman
St. Petersburg, Florida	Ludwig-Sky Harbor
Americus, Georgia	Souther
Augusta, Georgia	Bush
Douglas, Georgia	Municipal
Lansing, Illinois	Ford-Lansing
Indianapolis, Indiana	Sky Harbor
Davenport, Iowa	Cran
Wichita, Kansas	Municipal
Baton Rouge, Louisiana	E. Baton Rouge Parish
North Grafton, Massachusetts	North Grafton
Lansing, Michigan	Capitol City
Minneapolis, Minnesota	Victory
Clarksdale, Mississippi	Fletcher
Madison, Mississippi	Augustine
Cape Girardeau, Missouri	Harris
Kansas City, Missouri	Municipal
Robertson, Missouri	Municipal
Sikeston, Missouri	Harvey Park
Helena, Montana	Municipal
Omaha, Nebraska	Municipal
Reno, Nevada	Reno
Readington, New Jersey	Solberg-Hunterton
Albuquerque, New Mexico	Army Air Field
Albany, New York	Albany
Rochester, New York	Municipal
White Plains, New York	Westchester County
Charlotte, North Carolina	Cannon
Akron, Ohio	Municipal
Cincinnati, Ohio	Lunkin
Muskogee, Oklahoma	Hat Box
Oklahoma City, Oklahoma	Cimarron
Ponca City, Oklahoma	Municipal
Portland, Oregon	Portland-Troutdale
Pittsburgh, Pennsylvania	Bettis
Bennettsville, South Carolina	Palmer
Camden, South Carolina	Woodward
Sioux Falls, South Dakota	Sioux
Jackson, Tennessee	McKellar
Union City, Tennessee	Embry-Riddle
Ballinger, Texas	Bruce
Corsicana, Texas	Corsicana
Cuero, Texas	Municipal
Fort Stockton, Texas	Gibbs
Fort Worth, Texas	Hicks
Houston, Texas	Municipal
Lamesa, Texas	Lamesa
San Antonio, Texas	Municipal
Stamford, Texas	Arledge
Vernon, Texas	Victory
Salt Lake City, Utah	Municipal No. 1
Alexandria, Virginia	Hybla Valley
Morgantown, West Virginia	Municipal

RECONSTRUCTION FINANCE CORPORATION

A DISPOSAL AGENCY DESIGNATED BY THE SURPLUS PROPERTY BOARD

14—2

Within weeks of the war's end, advertisements for surplus trainers began to appear in aviation enthusiast magazines. This September 1945 RFC ad from *Flying* magazine offered primary and basic trainers at discount prices and listed sales centers by state. *Armand H. Veronico Collection*

There was no sentimentality in disassembling old warplanes. This view shows the fate of an early B-17 during the scrapping operations at Albuquerque, New Mexico, in 1947. Large sheets of armor plate were used to chop up the airplanes into manageable pieces that were fed into large aluminum smelters. *Kirtland AFB Historian's Office via H. M. Davidson*

Between 1945 and June 1947, the RFC and the War Assets Administration (WAA), which supplanted the RFC in March 1946, processed approximately 61,600 aircraft, of which nearly 26,900, primarily combat types, were sold for scrapping and 34,700 were sold for flyable purposes.[9] By June 1947, 40 percent of the U.S. civil aircraft fleet consisted of war surplus, primarily light aircraft of the utility and trainers types.[10]

The AAF and USN also released a large number of aircraft for disposal at overseas locations, avoiding the cost of bringing war-weary types back to the United States only to be scrapped. The overseas disposal program was administered by the U.S. Foreign Economic Administration (FEA), but was usually conducted by local military commanders. Many excess aircraft were made unflyable (usually using explosives) by military authorities at depot locations and abandoned to local scrap dealers. There were also numerous instances of local commanders ordering the bulldozing, burying, or sinking of their surplus airplanes. Any detailed information about overseas disposal practices was scattered in the postwar chaos.

The Development of an
Aircraft Disposal Policy

The specific policy toward the disposal of surplus aircraft was largely developed out of a study undertaken in late 1943. The Special Projects Office of AAF engaged the Harvard University Graduate

Bush Field, Augusta, Georgia, was the site of another storage field. XP-60C-CU, serial number 42-79424, traces its origins back to the P-40 through the P-46 and P-53. The XP-60C was powered by an R-2800-53 driving two counter-rotating propellers. Only three XP-60s were built and they were quickly scrapped at the end of the war. *Bernard Schulte*

School of Business Administration to analyze the problems of surplus aircraft disposal and make recommendations. The resulting report, "Disposal of Surplus Aircraft and Major Components Thereof," was completed in May 1944 and became widely known as the Harvard Report.[11]

Earlier, in February 1944, President Franklin D. Roosevelt established the Surplus War Property Administration (SWPA) as a planning body under the Office of War Mobilization and Reconversion. One of the SWPA's first actions was to set up an interdepartmental committee to obtain the best possible guidance in establishing overall aircraft disposal policy. The State, War, and Navy Departments were represented, as were the RFC and the Civil Aeronautics Administration (CAA). The new committee was headed by I. Welch Pogue, chairman of the Civil Aeronautics Board. The results of the Harvard study

were incorporated into the committee's examination of the problems of aircraft disposal. The Pogue Committee also issued a report that, with the earlier study, was used to set SWPA policy for aircraft and aircraft parts.

The Harvard group performed a detailed study of the American surplus aircraft experience that occurred at the end of World War I. There was major concern that much of the lack of American aviation development that plagued the 1920s was a direct result of the ample supply of World War I surplus equipment. This was particularly felt in the area of aircraft engines. The Harvard Report noted that more than 11,900 new Liberty engines were on hand at the conclusion of World War I, and that military budget limitations and the supply of stored engines forced aircraft designers to build new airframes around the old engine, thus choking off engine development.

Although the Army was happy to have such a large engine inventory in 1919, by 1925 the supply was an overwhelming burden as it was difficult to procure new engines with unused Liberty engines still available.[12] As late as 1930, World War I–era engines were still being carried on military stock lists and used in operational aircraft. With the military unable to procure new engines, the development of American liquid-cooled aircraft engines lagged behind those of other nations.[13]

The surplus pool of aircraft and equipment was held as detrimental to the development of both civil and military aviation and imposed a severe liability to U.S. aircraft manufacturers trying to find a market for new products. Of the 12,500 surplus World War I American aircraft, half were sold to civil dealers and individuals or transferred to other government agencies. With cheap airplanes and engines available, civil aviation enjoyed a boom; however, aircraft manufacturers were all but destroyed. Surplus airplanes that remained in the military inventory were used through the 1920s, also impacting the aircraft manufacturing industry with little market for new products.[14] The mainstay of the Army fleet between 1919 and 1925 was the DeHavilland DH-4, the majority of which had been placed in postwar storage and formed the pool for "new" equipment during the 1920s. As late as 1926, DH-4s were being withdrawn from storage, overhauled and modified, and then placed into service. In 1927, National Guard units still operated 140 Curtiss JN-4 Jennies of World War I vintage.[15]

For post–World War II planning, it was thus perceived that the sale of surplus planes and engines at extremely low prices was a threat to the national aircraft industry, and that a large inventory of surplus tactical aircraft would make it difficult to obtain authorization to purchase new equipment. During World War II, the aircraft industry had become an extremely valuable American asset and one that the policy planners felt was irreplaceable. The report noted that the maintenance of American airpower

As newer B-17Fs and Gs entered combat, earlier aircraft were relegated to training duties and eventually scrapped when they became so far removed from front-line aircraft. B-17Bs 39-01 and 38-212 have been put out to pasture at Lowry Field in 1943. B-17B, 39-01 was christened *The Goldbrick. William T. Larkins*

Boeing 314B NC18609 was delivered to Pan American in May 1941. It was impressed into service by the Navy and, at the end of the war, was stored at Floyd Bennett Field, New York. NC18609 was sold by the WAA in 1946 to Universal Airlines, which bought this and six other 314s for $352,000. The flying boat was later damaged in a storm and scrapped. *Harold G. Martin*

Factory-fresh P-51Ds line the ramp at Kelly AFB, San Antonio Air Material Area. These aircraft were quickly put to use during the Korean War. *National Archives*

depended on a healthy aviation industry, requiring promotion of both civil and military aviation. A healthy aviation industry would also provide high postwar employment but depended on the expansion of prewar civilian markets and the creation of new markets for private industry.[16]

Other areas of study concentrated on the logistical and budgetary limitations of trying to deal with the vast numbers of aircraft and parts expected to be surplus at the conclusion of the war. Also noted in the reports as an area of great concern were the distribution of surplus materials to other countries and the political administration of such transfers.

As a method to classify the types of surplus aircraft material, the Harvard Report divided surplus equipment into five classes, as indicated in Table 1. This classification system was carried forth and used through the disposal program.

When placed into the Harvard Report's time frame (May 1944), outlines of the developing aircraft disposal policy can be seen. Much of the report

Rows of tired B-17s, B-25s, and B-26s line the fields surrounding the Cal-Aero Flight Academy near Ontario, California, in 1946. The facility is now operated as the Chino Airport and has become, ironically, an internationally known center of vintage airplane restoration and operation. *William T. Larkins*

concentrated on the political aspects of the process as they applied to foreign relations, dealing with aircraft operated under Lend-Lease, and setting a pricing policy for domestic and foreign sales. A few of the conclusions of the Harvard Report are as follows:

The War, Navy, and State Departments should have the objective of using surplus disposal as a positive instrument to create sound foreign relations and future trade, especially export trade which may expand United States productive capacity.

After the Army Air Force has declared a given number of planes in a particular theater "surplus" and the War Department specifies no other military need for them, all the used planes should be surveyed at location . . . a substantial proportion of the surplus should be salvaged at location . . .

. . . lend-lease transport models, insofar as practicable, be nominally repossessed . . . The

---

Table 1[1]

Major Disposal Categories

Class A   Tactical aircraft, including heavy trainers. Useful for military purposes only.

Class B   Transport aircraft. Primarily useful for scheduled transport service.

Class C   Personal aircraft, including primary trainers. Adaptable to personal flying, fixed base operations, training, and miscellaneous uses.

Class D   Aircraft equipment and components. Of general use for military and commercial uses.

Class E   Unabsorbed surplus. All planes and components not useful for flight purposes.

[1] "Surplus Property," p. 73.

Over 1,300 aircraft were brought to Cal Aero Field by the RFC beginning in 1945. In June 1946 the field was sold by auction to the Sharp and Fellows Construction Company. *William T. Larkins*

A dramatic view of P-38s and B-24s parked along the fence at Cal-Aero in 1946. *William T. Larkins*

ultimate world distribution of United States transport models should be related to peacetime need and national policy rather than the chance result . . .

Surplus Class A planes should be held at foreign bases until agreements on international policies, if any, are concluded. Only after it becomes clear that planes will not be sold in the export market should these planes be placed in class E, where they will be held for nonflight educational or exhibitional use, broken down into useful components, or scrapped.[17]

Douglas A-20 Havocs settled onto their tails without the weight of their Wright R-2600 engines. These aircraft were cut up and smelted in late 1946 or early 1947 after the WAA sold the airfield. *William T. Larkins*

The conclusions drawn by the Pogue Committee Report were the basis for much of the policy set by the SWPA and Surplus Proptery Board (SPB). It suggested that every effort should be made to find uses for surplus aircraft. Pursuing an orderly disposal process and satisfying market needs were legitimate goals. However, tactical aircraft were expected to be "so war-weary, or so obsolete, that they will have no military or other appreciable value."[18] After all the aviation needs were met, there would still be large surpluses, which were to be distributed as needed for "educational, experimental, memorial and miscellaneous nonaviation uses."[19] The report recommended that any surplus aircraft or materials remaining be scrapped, and summed up its conclusions by stating: "Most important is the necessity of preserving as a national asset the capacity of our permanent aircraft manufacturing industry for research, development, and production of aircraft and aeronautical devices of the very latest types. Air power is today the key to national security."[20]

The Problem of Tactical Aircraft

In July 1944, in the course of studying the most efficient and cost-effective way of disposing of surplus aircraft, the AAF brought a war-weary B-24 to Patterson Field, near Dayton, Ohio, for a special project. The B-24 was towed into a hangar and a crew of mechanics broke the bomber down into its smallest component parts. Careful time records were kept to document the required man-hours, and at the completion of the disassembly process the resulting parts were spread across the hangar floor.

Representatives of various industries were brought in to examine the material and determine whether a use could be found for any of the parts. The overall conclusion was that, while some parts were usable, it was cheaper and safer for manufacturers to purchase new items for their products. Little beyond scrap value could be found for the remains of the B-24. It was found that 782.51 man-hours were expended to break the bomber down at a total labor cost of $3,200. The resulting 32,759 pounds of material was worth $2,400 in components and scrap. Thus, it was determined that the most cost-effective method of disposal was recovering the aluminum and other metallic content for a variety of uses.[21]

The disposal of tactical, or Class A, aircraft was considered to be a major problem through most of

Most of the C-27s in storage, including 90-0172 from the 24th Wing, Panama Canal Zone, are expected to be transferred to the U.S. State Department for service in Third World countries. Seven were in storage in March 2000. *Nicholas A. Veronico*

The U.S. Navy used the TC-4C to train A-6 Intruder bombardier/navigators. Closest to the camera, 852 and 853 were last flown by VA-128 and both entered storage on September 13, 1995. Aircraft with buzz numbers 575, 577, and the last on the row, 574, flew with VA-42 and were retired by September 1994. *Nicholas A. Veronico*

the studies as it was presumed that these aircraft were fundamentally unsalable. In a special report to Congress on November 23, 1945, titled "Aircraft and Aircraft Parts," the Surplus Property Administration (SPA) examined in detail the process of disposal for all classes of aircraft. However, with regard to tactical aircraft, it identified some limited uses in foreign military forces and a specialized demand in the civil fleet, but anticipated a huge unabsorbed surplus. Although the report significantly overestimated the actual number of surplus tactical airplanes, it clearly established the policy toward Class A aircraft, which was quickly implemented. The report projected that 89,200 tactical aircraft would be surplus by June 1946, with an inventory value of $12.9 billion.[22] (The actual number of combat aircraft released to the RFC, thus excluding overseas disposals, was closer to 27,000.[23])

In the November 1945 report, the SPA identified three possible areas of utilization for surplus tactical aircraft. First, with regard to foreign military usage, it outlined a policy whereby the War, Navy, and State Departments would advise the SPA from time to time of the types of aircraft that could be transferred to designated governments.[24]

Also examined was the commercial use of surplus airplanes. The report noted that the RFC had asked the military service which aircraft could be sold into the civil fleet without endangering national security and listed those aircraft as potentially available for sale. It was next determined if the CAA would, in fact, certify any of the warplanes for civil use. The report noted that "almost all the combat types so far put up for test have been rejected for certification and it is probable that almost all other combat types would also be rejected."[25] However, it was stated that this should not preclude the sale of these aircraft as there were certification options with restricted or experimental licenses. Also, it was felt that there was a very limited market in commercial schools, movie work, aerial photography, and advertising, and that every attempt should be made to sell into this market to accomplish some economic good.[26]

Finally, educational, memorial, and experimental uses were considered. On May 12, 1945, the SPB had initiated a successful program whereby qualifying educational institutions could obtain aircraft for a nominal fee. It was later widened to include experimental and memorial use. Several hundred surplus aircraft were released to educational institutions and, by late 1945, there was an increasing number of tactical aircraft also being transferred to communities for war memorials. The SPB and RFC sought to encourage such transfers.[27]

However, after all of these uses were considered, it was obvious that there was going to be a large amount of unabsorbed surplus. The report considered three alternatives. First was the possibility of storing and maintaining the aircraft. In August 1945, it was estimated to cost $20 per aircraft per month for storage. Even if the storage cost could be halved in 1946, the report projected that it would still require $25 million per year to store tactical aircraft.[28] Doing the arithmetic, the annual cost cited must have presumed the need to store 200,000 aircraft, which was wildly beyond the numbers expected. Nonetheless, the report soundly rejected any proposals to store and maintain the wartime fleet for a future use.

Another suggested alternative was abandoning the aircraft at the storage depots, but this was quickly rejected because it was contrary to the stated intent of the Surplus Property Act of 1944. Also, surplus tactical aircraft represented a "mine above ground"[29] resource in the form of aluminum scrap and other strategic materials. There were estimated to be hundreds of millions of pounds of aluminum alone. It was considered to be in the best interest of the government to try and recover some of its investment in tactical aircraft by making the scrap available for recovery and reuse.[30]

The obvious option was to position the aircraft for eventual scrapping and smelting and this became the announced policy of the SPA. Most components would not be salvaged because the amount of salvaged material would be far in excess of any perceived use. Scrapping operations had already been ordered in September 1944 when overseas commanders were ordered to salvage and scrap on site any tactical aircraft declared surplus in their jurisdiction. The scrapping program had been extended to domestic storeyards in June 1945 by Special Order 11 issued

Almost 40 Titan II missiles are in storage at AMARC. These nuclear-capable missiles will be used as bargaining chips at future arms reduction talks. *Nicholas A. Veronico*

Most of these Grumman S-2G Trackers seen in May 1996 have been allocated to the U.S. Department of Agriculture for future use as sprayers or tankers. *Nicholas A. Veronico*

by the SPA.[31] The record, however, does not indicate that any wholesale airfield scrapping operations began until early 1946.

Studies were conducted by the SPA on how best to perform the scrapping task. Salvage and scrapping experts, along with representatives of the Army, Navy, and aluminum industry, were gathered into an interdepartmental committee. Three conclusions were reached: that the materials contained in unsalable aircraft were a national asset to be preserved; that the scrapping and smelting effort was too expensive and duplicative for the government to conduct; and that the recovery of aluminum should be metered to allow gradual absorption by commercial users.[32]

The tactical aircraft scrapping policy was clearly articulated to the public by a number of pamphlets including one December 1945 document entitled *White Elephants With Wings* published by the SPB. It was

Acres of A-7 Corsair IIs and F-4 Phantoms fill the frame. The Phantoms will soon become full-scale aerial target drones. *Nicholas A. Veronico*

designed to educate the public on what was going to happen to the aircraft and explain the basis for this policy. A telling statement from the pamphlet reveals that "the fear of airpower strategists is that taxpayers, seeing thousands of surplus warplanes parked on airfields all over the country, will ask 'Why not use these planes before we buy more?' "[33] It concludes by stating:

"With the end of the war, there will soon be war-weary and obsolete aircraft stacked wing to wing on many airfields. Some of them will glisten when the sun shines on them and it will be hard to believe that they cannot be used. But they will have been condemned only after every practical use has been studied. They will be awaiting the day when manpower is available to take them apart and put their metal back into use . . ."[34]

Organizing for Aircraft Disposal

Even while policy was being formulated, the federal government was organizing for war surplus disposal. Beginning in January 1944, the administration of the disposal program was conducted by the CAA, largely because the fleet of War Training Service and other training aircraft under the jurisdiction of the CAA was deemed excess to the war effort. This fleet numbered approximately 5,000 aircraft and had been sold in individual sales by December 1944.[35]

As noted earlier, President Roosevelt created the Surplus War Property Administration in February 1944. The SWPA was an interim planning organization to function while awaiting Congressional legislation that would formally establish a federal disposal agency. SWPA designated various existing federal agencies as the disposal administrator for a particular class of property, whether it be aircraft, production plants, or real estate. On April 21, 1944, SWPA Regulation 1 designated disposal agencies and established surplus declaration and disposal procedures. The RFC was designated the disposal agency for surplus aircraft and parts within the continental United States, while the Treasury Procurement Division was the designated agency for aircraft within U.S. territories and possessions. The FEA was charged with disposal of aircraft and parts overseas in non-combat

Martin EB-57E, 55-4298, was equipped for electronic warfare operations and is believed to be only 1 of 25 EB-57Es. This aircraft last served with the 17th Defense Systems Evaluation Squadron and was retired to Davis-Monthan on July 26, 1979. It was sold to National Aircraft in Tucson in June 1995 and it is reported that the aircraft's cockpit still exists. *Nicholas A. Veronico*

The ZPG-3W was a post–World War II airborne, early-warning blimp. Bu.No. 144243 is one of only four built, and is the sole survivor. *Nicholas A. Veronico*

A number of educational institutions received aircraft for their apprentice programs. The University of Southern California acquired 12 aircraft in November 1945 for its Santa Maria, California, technical school. In this August 9, 1949, photo are (from left to right): BT-13B, 42-89652; C-46A, 42-3656; P-47D, 42-23278; P-59A, 44-22614—now at the March Field Museum, Riverside, California; P-38J, 44-23314; P-63A, 42-68894; and B-17F, 42-6073. In the background, but hard to see, is an AT-6, UC-78, and B-25. *William T. Larkins*

areas, while the military services were responsible for that task in their combat areas.

With its initial designation as the disposal agency for most of the domestic surplus property, the RFC began to organize an elaborate network of offices within its confines to administer the program. This agency had originally been established in early 1932 as a Depression-related agency to administer a variety of federal recovery programs. The RFC had built a number of domestic military bases during the war, and with its tentacles through the numerous aspects of the American economy, lent itself to the surplus disposal process. Its administration of surplus military bases also provided airfields for assembly, sales, storage, and disposal of aircraft. The RFC initially delegated the disposal task to its subsidiary Defense Plants Corporation, which assumed all disposal functions from the CAA by November 1944.[36]

Congressional endorsement of the SWPA efforts were carried forth in legislation approved on October 3, 1944, and entitled "The Surplus Property Act of 1944." It set forth the general disposal policy goals of the government in lengthy and complicated legislation. Essentially it established a three-member SPB which took over the jurisdiction of the SWPA. The Surplus Property Act left to the SPB the formulation of general policy and controls of disposal, and directed the SPB to designate disposal agencies within the federal establishment. The disposal agencies were to form their own policies as to the disposal of their assigned property. It is important to note that the SPB was charged only with the administration of general policy and was not involved in any specific disposal process.[37]

On January 24, 1945, the SPB established an advisory board for aircraft disposal with representatives

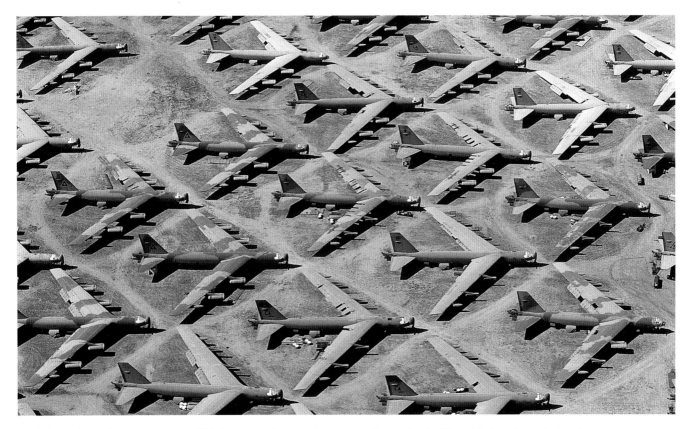

B-52Gs as far as the eye can see. This May 1996 aerial shows a portion of the B-52s yet to be eliminated under the Strategic Arms Reduction Treaty (START). *Nicholas A. Veronico*

of nineteen concerned governmental agencies. Included were members of the Civil Aeronautics Board, the Navy and War Departments, the RFC, and the FEA.[38] The Board began the process of creating regulations and special orders that sought to implement the new aircraft disposal policies. Many of the regulations duplicated or superseded earlier SWPA regulations. The RFC and FEA were retained as the disposal agency for the majority of aircraft and aircraft parts located, respectively, domestically and overseas.[39]

The SPB became the SPA by legislation passed on September 18, 1945. While the organizational body of the new Administration was widened in scope and manpower, the policy charge remained the same: the establishment and prosecution of the overall disposal policy of the federal government.

For the RFC, the organization of the aircraft disposal function changed continuously. However, by the end of 1945 it was becoming evident that the

The original *Outhouse Mouse* was a B-17G-25-BO, serial number 42-31636, that flew with the 91st Bomb Group's 323rd Bomb Squadron. *Outhouse Mouse II*, a B-52G, serial number 57-6508, last flew with the 2nd Bomb Wing, and arrived at AMARC on July 22, 1992. *Nicholas A. Veronico*

A good name with historic nose art can be a good luck charm. *Memphis Belle III* did not survive the scrapper's torch like her World War II B-17 namesake. *Nicholas A. Veronico*

Lucky 13 was B-29 Superfortress, seen having its protective cocoon removed at Warner Robins in the late 1940s. *National Archives*

administration of the program was becoming cumbersome due to jurisdictional conflicts of internal offices and divisions. To solve some of the internal problems, the RFC transferred all of its disposal functions into a subsidiary agency, the War Assets Corporation (WAC), on January 15, 1946.[40]

In March 1946, President Harry Truman streamlined all the government's disposal organizations by creating the WAA and bringing together the disposal functions of the RFC and the administration functions of the SPB. The WAA would remain the domestic surplus disposal agency until usurped by the General Services Administration in 1949. The WAA created the Office of Aircraft Disposal and the Surplus War Aircraft Division to administer the surplus aircraft program.

Aircraft Disposal Policy Implemented

The military, particularly the AAF, had been dealing with surplus aircraft since 1943. Most of the equipment was war-weary veterans that began to accumulate at overseas bases as new equipment arrived in various theaters. After September 1944, the

Lucky 13 was also worn on a B-52G, 58-0236, last operated with the 2nd Bomb Wing and entered storage on October 13, 1992. The Stratofortress was eliminated under START, shortly after this May 1996 photo was taken. *Nicholas A. Veronico*

B-52G, 59-0249 is a veteran of the 379th Bomb Group and arrived for storage on September 10, 1991. The cockpit wall has been cut out to preserve the aircraft's nose art, which was turned over to the Air Force Museum by AMARC. *Nicholas A. Veronico*

FEA began to administer a program to salvage and scrap surplus combat aircraft at overseas locations.[41] The FEA, created in September 1943, administered the U.S. Lend-Lease program overseas.[42] Presumably, it was the Lend-Lease connection that placed overseas disposal under the FEA. The FEA was eliminated in September 1945 and replaced by the new Office of Foreign Liquidation under the Department of State.[43] The Foreign Liquidations Commissioner administered the overseas disposal program.

Beginning in 1944, domestic aircraft declared excess to military needs were turned over to the RFC for disposal. The RFC established domestic storage and sales centers, and by August 1945, 30 sales-storage depots and 34 sales centers were in operation. Each sales-storage depot, located primarily on surplus military fields (the RFC also was

Old Crow Express was named after a World War II B-17 from the 303rd Bomb Group. This B-52G, 57-6492, was last flown by the 379th Bomb Group and has been scrapped. *Nicholas A. Veronico*

Ex-93rd Bomb Wing B-52G, 58-0167, awaits its final fate, having survived at AMARC into the new millennium. This aircraft has yielded many parts for the remaining flyable B-52s since its May 28, 1991, arrival at Davis-Monthan. *Nicholas A. Veronico*

designated the disposal agency for surplus real estate), and each sales center, which was located near a major market area, were operated by an RFC contractor and administered by an RFC field office.[44] For example, the RFC Oklahoma City Office's Aircraft Division administered two sales centers—Muskogee, Oklahoma, at Hat Box Airport and Cimarron Field near Oklahoma City; and two sales-storage depots at Ponca City Airport at Ponca City, and Searcy Field at Stillwater, Oklahoma.

After August 1945, the RFC decided to close all sales centers and concentrate salable surplus aircraft at five storage-sales depots. This decision was primarily taken to reduce storage costs and make it easier for purchasers to select aircraft.[45] However, the number of storage-sales depots was constantly changing through the last half of 1945. The military greatly increased its surplus declarations beginning in October 1945, and some sales centers apparently were not closed. By the end of 1945, the RFC was still operating 29 sales-storage depots across the country.[46]

The majority of the sales centers were organized for the disposal of Class C aircraft, composed of liaison, trainers, and utility cargo types, which were considered by the RFC as the most salable category for general disposal. However, tactical aircraft were also available. Established prices ranged from $450 for a BT-13 to $8,250 for a B-25 to $32,500 for a B-32. AT-6s were available for $1,500, while a P-38 was offered at $1,250 and a P-51 at $3,500. Purchase terms for veterans specified a 15 percent down payment for aircraft weighing more than 5,000 pounds and the loan was

The Consolidated B-32 Dominator was developed concurrently with the B-29. The B-32 had some teething troubles and was primarily flown as a crew trainer. This mix of slightly used and factory-fresh B-32s awaits the scrapper's torch at Walnut Ridge. *National Archives*

C-131E, 57-2552, was originally built as an electronic countermeasures trainer and was transferred to the USN early in its career as an R4Y-2, Bu.No. 145963. The aircraft last served with the 176th Tactical Fighter Squadron of the Wisconsin Air National Guard. The plane flew into AMARC on January 13, 1987. *Ron Strong*

carried at 4 percent per year. RFC advertisements for aircraft sales were run in aviation magazines on a continuing basis to spur the disposal of salable aircraft.[47] As noted earlier, approximately 35,000 surplus aircraft were ultimately sold for flyable purposes, most of these being light aircraft and trainers.

The storage lots were authorized to issue ferry permits to the owner's home base, after which the aircraft was grounded pending CAA certification. The CAA did not get involved at the storage depots, and the aircraft did not receive a CAA civil registration number until the new owner complied with required modifications and inspections.[48]

Class B aircraft, or the medium and heavy transports, were handled differently. Initially, beginning in July 1944, in-demand transport types such as the C-47 and C-54 were placed into an allocation program.

Purchase prices were established, which included conversion allowances for CAA certification, and were set based on the earning power of each type. Leasing arrangements were also available to allow quick use of surplus transports while awaiting new equipment from manufacturers. The SPB estimated, in November 1945, that 10,500 transport planes of all types would eventually be declared surplus.[49] The RFC decided that a number of these aircraft would be made available to foreign users, primarily to ensure usage of U.S. equipment overseas and broaden the demand for U.S.-manufactured products.[50] By mid-1947, 1,750 medium and heavy transports (C-46, C-47, and C-54s) had been sold to both domestic and foreign airlines. On March 31, 1947, 90 percent of the 256 DC-4s operating in the sole U.S. airline fleet had been converted from surplus C-54s.[51]

The Air Force Museum has control of more than 20 C-123s, many of them ex-*Ranch Hand* aircraft used to spray Agent Orange during the Vietnam War. *Ian Abbott*

Aircraft Disposal for Educational and Memorial Use

As noted earlier, the RFC initiated a program in May 1945 that provided for commercially worthless aircraft to be transferred to eligible educational institutions for technical programs. The first aircraft to be transferred was a war-weary B-17F that went to the Williamsport, Pennsylvania, Technical Institute.

Receiving schools had to pay transportation fees and a nominal disposal cost to obtain the aircraft. However, pricing policy provided a B-17 for $350, and a new Pratt & Whitney R-4360 radial engine was offered for $10. Central to the transfer of the aircraft was that the receiving institution had to sign a statement that the aircraft was for non-flight purposes and had to be rendered nonairworthy or dismantled prior to disposing of the aircraft.

In November 1945, the University of Southern California (USC) took advantage of the program and obtained 12 aircraft including a B-17, B-25, P-38, P-61, P-47, and a P-63. USC had the aircraft flown to Santa Maria Airport in Central California for use at its technical school.[52] In December 1945, the program was expanded to include a wide variety of public institutions, which enabled local municipalities to obtain aircraft for memorial use. Once again, a small transfer fee was required and the aircraft were allowed one-time ferry flights to their new owners. However, the scrapping provision was written into transfer arrangements that restricted any further sales without government approval.[53]

The Scrapping of Tactical Aircraft

The RFC dispersed a number of tactical, or Class A, aircraft at various depots around the country where

Yankee Doodle II was the last of 193 Boeing B-52Gs delivered to the Air Force. This plane was built at Boeing's Wichita, Kansas, assembly line and entered storage on October 27, 1992. It will eventually be eliminated to comply with START. *Ron Strong*

F-106A, 59-0130, arrived at Davis-Monthan on April 3, 1985, and was recycled into the F-106 drone program as QF-106A, AD152 to serve as an aerial target. *Ron Strong*

they were made available for sale. An investment partnership headed by movie pilot Paul Mantz completed the first field-size purchase in February 1946, when 478 aircraft at Stillwater, Oklahoma, were transferred. Most aircraft at Stillwater were scrapped, but a few survived for movie work. Other individual sales of surplus fighters and bombers from scattered RFC fields were recorded.

However, the RFC had concentrated most tactical aircraft at six storage depots located at Walnut Ridge, Arkansas; Kingman, Arizona; Ontario, California; Clinton and Altus, Oklahoma; and Albuquerque, New Mexico. General sales of these fighters and bombers were permitted under the

guidelines set by the RFC up until June 1946, when each of the major storage depots, with the exception of Altus, was put up for bid as scrap. The offering included 8,320 B-17s and B-24s, 7,188 fighters, and totaled 20,703 aircraft.[54] The advertisement for bids was made on June 10, 1946, and awarded on July 1, 1946. Within four months each of the fields had been turned over to private contractors that organized their own smelter operations. The original bid process required that the salvage and smelting be completed within 14 months of the bid award, and most firms had completed the job by the end of 1947. The rest is, as they say, history.

CHAPTER 2
Storage Depot 41: Kingman Army Air Field

It was commonplace during the immediate years following World War II to see concentrations of surplus military warplanes at almost every air base around the country. One of the more impressive sites in this regard, and the one location to receive the most media attention and attract the most controversy, was the former Kingman Army Air Field, Kingman, Arizona.

The origins of the Kingman Army Air Field (KAAF) date back to 1940 when the U.S. government began scouting locations for future training facilities. The remote, wide-open spaces of Kingman, Arizona, made it a logical candidate as a place where future B-17 gunners could be trained. In early 1942, a tract of land, bordered on one side by the famed Route 66, was officially selected by the AAF, and after a few months of construction the new Kingman Flexible Gunnery School was opened for business. During the war more than 36,000 airmen passed through KAAF as they received gunnery training.[55] Each gunner had to complete an intense curriculum that consisted of qualifying with BB guns, shotguns, and, finally, the .50-caliber machine guns that would be used on Boeing's Flying Fortresses. Gunnery instruction continued at KAAF until the end of the World War II. At that time, training activities started to wind down while the airfield itself began to take on its new role in the postwar world.

In the fall of 1945, the U.S. government was again looking for locations, but this time not for training purposes. The AAF possessed thousands of surplus airplanes and they needed a place to park them while government officials formulated postwar policy. Again, KAAF's large desert facility offered an ideal storage location. At first, the task of caring for the surplus warplanes was put under the control of the RFC. The RFC was the only government organization in the near-postwar period that was funded to advance the money needed to handle the storage and sales of surplus property.[56] The RFC selected Julian Q. Myers to run the storage operation in Kingman.

"I was the assistant manager and mechanic at Ontario Army Air Field," said Myers. "I got to messing around with the airplanes there (A-20s), and I became acquainted with the regional airport director in Los

There were more than 5,000 surplus combat aircraft stored at Kingman in June 1946. This number included approximately 2,567 B-24 Liberators, 1,832 B-17 Flying Fortresses, 678 P-38 Lightnings, 37 B-32 Dominators, 141 B-25 Mitchells, plus a few hundred Curtiss P-40s and Bell P-63s. *Robert A. Kropp Collection*

Boeing-built B-17G-35, serial number 42-31990, arrived in England on April 6, 1944. The bomber flew missions with the Eighth Air Force's 381st Bomb Group, 535th Bombardment Squadron, stationed at Ridgewell. The plane arrived at Kingman on February 26, 1946. *Robert A. Kropp Collection*

A Bell P-63 stripped of armament and wearing a civil registration awaits its pilot and a new home. *Robert A. Kropp Collection*

Angeles. One day he asked me to fly out to Kingman and talk to Col. Lance Call about what we wanted to do. The colonel didn't think so much of our storage plans, but we got an airplane and taxied it up to test our ideas and they worked out fine. In late September or early October, I signed a contract to take over Kingman. I hired some people and got things ready, and I managed to have a good solid crew on staff when the first airplanes started to arrive."[57] The RFC advanced Myers $50,000 a month to cover payroll and all the expenses of the Kingman facility.[58]

Myers' initial instructions were simple but difficult. "I was to pickle, preserve, and fix up all airplanes that had less than 100 hours on them," recalled Myers. "I was to really conserve them, which we did, and we had hundreds of them." The pickling process Myers mentioned required a great deal of work. Paper documentation was processed on every aircraft that landed at Kingman, and the star on each was painted out to show that it no longer belonged to the AAF. The engines on low-time aircraft were preserved in accordance with procedures that had been developed by the military. "We ran white lantern gas through every engine on the low-time airplanes in order to burn off any lead that had accumulated inside," said Myers. "I also had the crews squirt Shell oil compound into the carburetors to help preserve the internal parts. Some days I received over 100 airplanes to process, so I was ordering white gas by the 7,000-gallon tank car. The external parts of the engines were coated with protective Cosmolene grease and then covered with canvas. Lastly, we sealed each window before the plane was towed to its parking spot. It took eight men approximately one day to process a bomber, so we had a large backlog of airplanes that had to have their engines run every two weeks to keep them in peak condition."[59]

Myers was also receiving battle-weary B-17s and B-24s—some straight from overseas, in addition to the near-factory-fresh airplanes. Some of these bombers still carried the famous nose art that had made many of them household names in wartime America. At its peak, KAAF was reported to have more than 7,000 warplanes spread across more than five square miles of desert.[60] This massive collection of warbirds glistening in the bright Arizona sun certainly entertained many travelers passing through Kingman in the mid-to-late 1940s.

Myers was also in charge of setting up departments to sell complete airplanes, components, gasoline, and any other items that might bring a return on the government's wartime investment. "I had 26 brand-new Douglas A-26 airplanes come in that still had the paper on the seats and paper on the walls," said Myers. "They were supposed to go to the military but instead they came to me. We sold every one of them for $2,000 each."[61] The pricing schedule that the RFC used to sell its surplus aircraft was a little odd, to say the least. For example, one could buy a low-time Lockheed P-38 Lightning full of fuel for $1,250.[62] However, the purchase price for a P-38 propeller ran $3,800.[63] It is possible that the RFC used ths type of sales tactic to accelerate the disposal

Veteran of the Pacific Campaign, *Mabel's Labels* served with the 43rd Bomb Group on Ie Shima. The nose art has been attributed to an artist with the last name of Bartigan. *Robert A. Kropp Collection*

of its complete aircraft, but Myers has another possible explanation: "I believe it was two separate departments in Washington setting pricing policy without one talking to the other."[64] On the other hand, maybe the RFC knew something that wasn't really obvious to the casual observer of the time. For instance, many of the airlines were very interested in acquiring the new VHF radios that were installed in some of Kingman's fighters. But they didn't want to pay the inflated RFC component prices nor did they want to deal with disposing of what was left of the airframes after the items of interest had been removed. Forrest M. Bird, a former ferry pilot, took advantage of this very situation after he purchased 48 Lockheed Lightnings from Kingman. After removing the airplanes from the desert, he sold the radios to the airlines for more than the Lightnings' purchase price and then sold the P-38 airframes to individuals for approximately $900 each.[65] So maybe the RFC prices were not so odd after all.

The actual process of buying an airplane from the RFC at Kingman was easy. All one needed was the purchase price and enough time to sort through

An engineless *Gambler's Luck* brought her crew home safely. Her luck ran out at Kingman.
Robert A. Kropp Collection

thousands of airplanes that were stored there. Once the decision was made, the aircraft of choice was brought to the ramp, serviced, and readied for flight. Each purchase came with an automatic authorization from the CAA that allowed a pilot to fly the airplane from Kingman Field to one's home base. The process was simple and efficient, but apparently the RFC paid little attention to pilot qualification. Julian Myers explains: "Once an airplane left the field, we knew nothing about what happened to them except for a few. There was one guy who came and bought a P-38. Some of the salespeople asked me to talk to this fellow, because he didn't seem to have the experience to fly high-performance airplanes. I told him that it was really dangerous not to have the experience for it, but I couldn't do anything legally to stop him. So I gave him my parachute and told him to go ahead and fly it to Washington state. We were all scared to death but somehow he got the plane off the runway. He later

returned my parachute with a letter explaining what had happened on his trip home: He lost his hydraulic system somewhere over Oregon and had to hand-crank the gear down. He then landed with no flaps on a small airfield that was better suited for a J-3 Cub. After fixing the airplane he managed to get home. He also told me in his letter that his total flying experience was but a few hours in a Waco UPF-7."[66]

A number of fighter warbirds that exist today were purchased from Kingman in the early-to-mid-1946 period. In stark contrast, hardly any of the KAAF bombers managed to escape their unfortunate fate. The B-17s and B-24s did carry an expensive price tag of $13,750, but there just wasn't a market for the heavy bombers.[67] However, a few of Kingman's more famous bombers were set aside to be used as war memorials. "We delivered one airplane to the city of Los Angeles, California," said Myers. "This was the *Swoose*. We got it ready, but the pilot

This is the image most people have of Kingman—B-17s as far as the eye can see. The majority of these aircraft were combat veterans returned from Europe. For additional information on the bomb groups identifiable in these photos, see Appendix IV: Larkins' Kingman Photograph Tables. *Mohave County Historical Society*

wouldn't accept it. 'We can't take that airplane,' said the pilot. 'It's got nice seats, and it has a nice paint job. That isn't the way we flew this airplane!' I got permission to repaint the airplane, take the seats out and put in the other old things, but the copilot still wasn't satisfied. He then took a crowbar and punched a hole in the fin. He said, 'Now that's more like what the flak did to this airplane.' The crew then flew the B-17 to California and it sat in Los Angeles and went to pieces."[68] Another B-17 that should have survived its stay at Kingman was the 5,000th Boeing B-17 *5 Grand*. This famous Flying Fortress was sent to war with the 96th Bomb Group in England, carrying on its aluminum skin the signatures of the employees who built the airplane at Boeing's Seattle plant.[69] According to Myers, a man was sent to Arizona to inspect the B-17, but after seeing the bomber he got

disgusted because someone had removed his name from the Flying Fortress. So he went back to Seattle, and no one ever heard from him again. Sadly, *5 Grand* would later be cut up and melted down.

In mid-January 1946, Kingman's surplus disposal organization was put under control of the newly established WAC, which later became the WAA. The military officially decommissioned KAAF in February 1946 and all of its facilities were given over to the WAA, which referred to the Kingman operation as their "Storage Depot 41."[70]

The sales of airworthy aircraft continued while the WAA looked for a more cost-effective way to dispose of its surplus airplanes. The idea of offering entire fields of surplus airplanes for competitive bid eventually won favor with the WAA, and in June 1946 the sale of individual aircraft was completely

continued on page 39

The 5,000th Seattle-built B-17 since the beginning of the war, a B-17G-70-BO, serial 43-437716, was rolled out on May 13, 1944, adorned with the signatures of those who built her. Christened *5 Grand*, the bomber served in the 8th Air Force with the 96th Bomb Group's 338th Bombardment Squadron. The plane flew 78 combat missions and its crews accounted for two German fighters. After the war, *5 Grand* was returned stateside and received a hero's welcome when it returned to Seattle. The city attempted to secure the plane but could not come up with funding and *5 Grand*, like so many other B-17s, was recycled in the Kingman smelters. *Boeing Historical Archives (top) and William T. Larkins (bottom)*

An aerial view of the Kingman ramp on February 8, 1947. Scrapping operations are not yet in full swing. Three B-17s, two without engines, one B-24, and six engineless single-tail B-24Ns can be seen on the ramp in the foreground. The three smelters are located at the end of the tarmac. *William T. Larkins*

Lockheed P-38s without radiators or engines sit on their tails awaiting the scrapper's chopping blade. *Carlos Elmer via Mohave County Historical Society*

This is the most surprising of the photos taken by William T. Larkins in February 1947. Larkins had not looked at the negative until 1999, and when he did, he discovered 107 P-38s. In the photograph, Larkins saw 56 P-38s lined up near the railroad tracks in seven rows: Row 1 has 16, Row 2 has 14, Row 3 has 4, Row 4 has 5, Row 5 has 9, Row 6 has 5, and Row 7 has 3. The amazing thing is that Row 2 has 14 all-black P-38M night fighters! Even more interesting are three rows of P-38s tucked underneath the wings of the second B-24 group from the right. The first row has 16 planes, the second 18, and the third 14. *William T. Larkins*

Three smelters were built, one of which can be seen behind the B-24, to support the Kingman salvage operation. The units were operated around the clock and at the height of efficiency processed approximately 35 aircraft a day. *L. S. Youngblood*

Continued from page 35

discontinued at Depot 41. A 17-year-old pilot named Bill Lear Jr., son of William P. Lear Sr.—founder of Lear Jet—just happened to arrive at Kingman a day after the WAA decided to close down its airworthy aircraft sales. Lear had always wanted to fly a P-38 so he hitchhiked to Kingman after learning that the WAA was selling low-time Lightnings for $1,250.[71] He carried with him a check that his dad had written to cover the price of the surplus craft. However, Lear received some very sad news shortly after he arrived at Depot 41. He missed it by a day! Lear's disappointment

Right: Wunderlich Construction brought several 40-ton Lima cranes to Arizona. The crane would lift and then drop a heavy metal blade above each aircraft in order to produce pieces small enough to charge the smelters. Here a B-17 wing meets its end. *L. S. Youngblood*

Below: The molten aluminum produced by the smelters was converted to 1,500-pound ingots that were later transported to aluminum process companies by railroad freight cars. *L. S. Youngblood*

Carpetbagger B-24M-31-FO, serial number 44-51505, flew night missions over occupied territory dropping leaflets and supplies to the resistance. Both the 8th and 15th Air Forces had Carpetbagger outfits.
William T. Larkins

monumental task less difficult. Eventually, my count of 5,483 airplanes was accepted by all concerned."[79]

In late August 1946, Martin Wunderlich received word that the WAA regional office in Los Angeles was seeking separate bids for the gasoline and oil stored in the Kingman airplanes. This information was somewhat confusing to Wunderlich as he believed that his bid had purchased these commodities with the planes, so he sent a message to the WAA in Washington, D.C. The WAA responded by sending the following dispatch to their office in Los Angeles: "All combat aircraft located at Kingman were offered as is, where is, which included gasoline in planes. High bidder figured gasoline, resulting in considerable higher return to Government; therefore, separate bids for gasoline cannot be considered."[80] On August 22, 1946, an article entitled "2,500,000 Gals. Gas Sold Twice By U.S." appeared in the *New York Times*. This exposé asserted that the WAA office in Los Angles was instructed to look for separate bids on approximately 3 million gallons of gasoline and oil left in the airplanes at Kingman. But after the bids started coming in, they were ordered by General James A. Mollison, WAA Deputy Administrator for Aircraft Disposal in Washington, to stop seeking separate bids on the grounds that the gasoline and oil were included with the purchase of the planes. It also noted that the WAA's original advertisements for the surplus airplanes said nothing about gasoline. Stories

that hint of possible government scandal usually receive national attention, and the Kingman gas story was no exception. Numerous newspapers around the country ran the story, which in due course attracted the attention of the Senate Investigation Committee. In the meantime, plans to salvage the airplanes at all five depots began to take shape.

Wunderlich Construction joined the winners of the other surplus depots to form a single salvage company called the Aircraft Conversion Company (ACC). This new organization was managed by Slim Dahlstrum (overall manager), J. E. Walters (production manager), and George Darneille (government liaison).[81] All three of these individuals had ties to the Texas Railway Equipment Company (TREC), which was owned by Brown and Root Construction of Houston, Texas. Having a general supervising company was a smart way to maximize profits by spreading the overhead expenses across the profits of five salvage operations. For example, ACC eventually built the 10 smelting furnaces and hired the metallurgist and other professional people who would share their time between Kingman, Walnut Ridge, and the like. It is also interesting to note that ACC/TREC received an additional $1,091,476.61 contract to supply the AAF with spare parts.[82] The AAF needed a source for components in order to support obsolete airplanes that had been sold to friendly foreign governments. If the required parts were not available

Where Ya Been, Old Girl?

Each of the warplanes at Kingman had stories to tell. This B-17G, carrying the Army serial number of 44-6315, is a good example. This airplane was built by the Douglas Aircraft Company at Long Beach, California, in June 1944. It was flown overseas and assigned to the 487th Bomb Group at Lavenham, England. Its first crew was led by pilot Jack Sadr and was named *Fearless Fosdick*. Fearless Fosdick was a character in the comic strip of the day, and nose art depicting Fosdick was added to both sides of the nose. Curiously, the artwork on the right side of the airplane carried the full name, while that on the left side apparently was incomplete, only the "F" of Fosdick being applied. Sadr and his crew flew it for a combat tour over Europe, one mission of which resulted in so much combat damage that the airplane was forced down in friendly territory in Belgium. A maintenance crew from the bomb group was flown in to repair the damage and the B-17 was eventually ferried back to its base. After Sadr's crew had completed its tour, *Fearless Fosdick* was assigned to a crew led by Donald Church. Church's copilot, Robert Browne, remembered *Fearless Fosdick* as "the most patched-up assembly of aluminum" he'd ever expected to see, with new patches applied over old patches. Don Church and his crew flew 34 additional missions in *Fearless Fosdick* between November 1944 and March 1945. At that point, Church's crew turned the B-17 over to a third crew led by pilot Chuck Hough. They evidently completed the war in *Fearless Fosdick* and flew the plane back to the United States in May 1945. All told, *Fearless Fosdick* was credited with 72 combat missions. The photo at right shows pilot Donald Church (left) with *Fearless Fosdick* at Lavenham in late 1944 and comes from the scrapbook of the crew's ball turret gunner, Corporal G. W. Wilson. The view below shows the airplane just over two years later, patiently awaiting a fiery and undignified end.
William T. Larkins

Famed Lockheed test pilot Tony LeVier (right) receiving the bill-of-sale documents from Julian Q. Myers (left). LeVier was the first person to purchase a surplus P-38 Lightning from Depot 41 in early 1946. *Lockheed*

airplane.[86] Desirable items such as a pistol no doubt found their way into the pockets of the lucky finder rather than being pitched on the ground for the warehouse crew. Other items were also removed from the field. "I met many characters in component sales while I was at Kingman," said Youngblood. "One of them remarked, 'Ninety-six percent of Americans are honest and the rest are in the aircraft business.' I think his observations had some merit. Some of the 4-percenters I mentioned earlier had contacts among the workers who would take items from the project and independently sell them to parts dealers. At unannounced times, the security people held a vehicle inspection for outgoing vehicles at shift change. The gate was approximately one-quarter mile from the parking area. As soon as the line started slowing, the occupants of the cars began jettisoning contraband on

the roadside. The company trucks would then gather the material and return it to the warehouse."[87]

Unspent .50-caliber shells were also searched out by the salvage crews. The smelters at Kingman were damaged more than once after live ordnance cooked off under the heat of the ovens. So measures were taken to extract volatile and hazardous materials from the fighters and bombers before they met their end in the smelters.

In 1947 the details concerning the sale of aircraft at Kingman came under the watchful eye of the Senate Investigating Committee. The so-called 2,500,000-gallon fuel story that made the papers in 1946 touched off several complaints from the unsuccessful bidders. For example, Kopelove Iron & Steel of Dayton, Ohio, bitterly complained: "We had no idea that the gasoline remained in the planes. Had we

One of the few North American Mustangs on the field was this RF-6C-10-NT, serial number 44-10911.
William T. Larkins

known there was gasoline in the planes we would undoubtedly have adjusted our bid according[ly]."[88] On June 4, 1947, the "Subcommittee of the Committee on Expenditure in the Executive Departments" began hearings in Washington, D.C., to determine if the WAA had given Wunderlich Construction some kind of unfair advantage during the bidding process. Senator Homer Ferguson presided while special counsel Miles Culehan handled some of the questioning. The investigation was one of explicit detail that took a lawyer's approach of dissecting every word that appeared in the documents of evidence. The committee went so far as to question if the WAA was charging Wunderlich Construction rent for the use of government-owned bed linen and silverware at Kingman. The Senate Investigating Committee, however, was mainly interested in determining if all the bidders were equally informed that the gas and oil stored inside each surplus aircraft were included in the bid price. In addition, they wanted to know how much fuel and lubricant were available to the high bidder

and what the return on investment might be. They were also very interested in determining exactly how many airplanes were sold to Wunderlich Construction in 1946.

A number of people were called to testify during the course of the three-day (June 4, 18, and 19) hearing, but possibly the most important person to appear before the investigating body was Gen. James A. Mollison. General Mollison explained that all of the bidders were informed that the airplanes were to be sold "as is, where is" and that included the oil and gas in each plane. He went on to add: "We took the position all along in the Office of Aircraft Disposal that the gasoline went with the planes. The Los Angeles regional office took the position that the gasoline was theirs."[89] Senator Ferguson followed the general's statement with several pointed questions related to why the WAA in Los Angeles didn't know about the fuel. He also read portions of several letters that his committee had received from bidders who felt they had been deceived by the WAA back

The RFC was eager to distribute surplus warplanes to any community or organization that wanted war memorials. This B-17D, better known as the *Swoose*, was transferred to the city of Los Angeles in 1946 at the encouragement of one of its wartime pilots, Col. Frank Kurtz. After paying a nominal transfer fee, the city took possession of the airplane in a ceremony held at Mines Field in Los Angeles in April 1946. Kurtz flew the veteran of the early, dark days of the Pacific War on its delivery flight from the War Assets field at Kingman, Arizona. This view shows the B-17D as displayed at the Los Angeles Airport. *William T. Larkins*

in 1946. General Mollison could not explain the communication breakdown between the two offices, but he did tell his interrogator why the WAA didn't investigate the so-called gasoline scandal. "It is pretty hard, Senator, to read the minds of these people if they don't come to me and tell me that they feel they have been discriminated against," said Mollison. "That would have been the time for them to speak up rather than a year later. These people never, so far as I know, presented this picture to me before. It was my understanding that everybody was perfectly happy at that time."[90]

The quantity of gas and oil at Kingman came up repeatedly throughout the hearings, as well. At one point Senator Ferguson directed the following question to General Mollison: "At the time you sold these airplanes, did you know that they had gasoline and oil in them of the value, more than, or as much, or nearly as much as he (Wunderlich) was paying for them?"[91] General Mollison estimated that the warplanes at Kingman contained 2,000,000 gallons of

fuel that was valued at only $50,000—a far cry from the almost $3 million that Wunderlich paid out for 5,483 airplanes. "The gasoline matter received much publicity," recalled Lindsey Youngblood. "One magazine alleged that Wunderlich had received enough from the sale of fuel to pay for the planes. This was nonsense. Wunderlich made less than $20,000 gross on the fuel. It was a nuisance to us. We sent samples to Wright Field, but the Air Force wasn't interested because of the varnish that had accumulated in the fuel. The senators made a big deal out of gasoline, engine oil, hydraulic fluid, and brake fluid. Talk about splitting hairs! The Congressional Committee went to unsuccessful bidders after the fact and asked loaded questions such as, 'Would you have bid more had you known about the fuel?' Of course the answer would be 'Yes!' They wouldn't admit to bidding blind and poorly. Any intelligent bidders would have examined the planes closely enough to have an idea about the amount of fuel and other details at a project that large."[92]

The *Swoose* was stored outdoors at the National Air and Space Museum's facility at Suitland, Maryland, from 1961 until the mid-1970s. It was then disassembled for indoor storage, as shown in this February 1989 view. Finally, after nearly five decades of storage, it is slated to be placed on public display at the new NASM annex being constructed at the Washington Dulles Airport when that facility opens in 2003. Although not scheduled for restoration, the historic B-17D will nonetheless be available as a public memorial, the original intent of the RFC when it was transferred to the city of Los Angeles in 1946. *A. Kevin Grantham*

The myth surrounding the Kingman gasoline has long survived the airplanes that perished there. Stories of how each warplane was topped off with fuel before it was parked in the desert and tales of the vast profits that were made on the Kingman gasoline are legendary. However, are they true? Julian Myers was involved with the Kingman salvage project from the beginning to the end, and he, like Youngblood, also says, "No!"

"There wasn't a tremendous amount of fuel left," said Myers. "The planes didn't come in with that much to begin with. Everyone was mistaken about that because the Air Force was putting just enough fuel in the planes to get them to Kingman, and they often miscalculated because a number of them ran out. A B-24 went down in the desert, and I had to go

get that one. Many times there wasn't enough fuel left in an arriving plane to taxi it to its parking spot. We didn't service any airplane that came into the field. They were stored with what was in them."[93]

The Senate Committee raised additional questions about the mistakes the WAA had made in counting the airplanes stored at Kingman. The basic confusion came from conflicting numbers (5,443 vs. 5,483) taken from separate inventories. The 5,443 figure included in the WAA 1946 advertisements was derived from a May 16, 1946, inventory.[94] The 5,483 figure came from a WAA memorandum dated June 14, 1946.[95] Col. John Carey, deputy administrator in charge of the WAA Office of Aircraft and Electronics Disposal, testified that several inventories were made

Preserving Kingman's Legacy on Film

By William T. Larkins

Kingman Army Air Field, three miles northeast of Kingman, Arizona, is better known today for its postwar operation as an aerial junkyard than for its original purpose as an advanced training field. This large base was at one time a four-engine copilot (B-17) school, as well as a flexible gunnery school, operating under the Western Flying Training Command.

With the end of the war and with no further need for advanced flight training, the AAF field was closed. This coincided with the need for a large area with good weather to temporarily store large numbers of war surplus aircraft. The operation was begun under the WAA, but was soon changed to that of a private contractor when the Wunderlich Contracting Company was awarded the bid to process some 5,000 aircraft for scrap metal.

Thus, by the time I got there on February 6, 1947, it had become a private operation. This is one of the reasons why it was so hard to get into—there was no appealing through channels to government offices, it was strictly dealing directly with a hard-headed junk dealer not in the least bit interested in history or crazy collectors. It didn't take me long to find this out, for after driving 562 miles from San Francisco in my well-worn 1932 Model B Ford, I was told flatly that my prior request to the WAA didn't mean a thing. This was now a private operation and they did not want people wandering about the field stealing things.

After considerable arguing and pleading, a compromise was finally reached. If I would pay the wages of a guard to accompany me at all times, and agree to stay out of the aircraft, I would be permitted to photograph there for a day. This turned out to be a blessing in disguise, although I didn't realize it at the time. It actually provided me with a jeep and driver for the day. The area was so large, and time so short, that if I had been on my own it would have resulted in my getting fewer photos. With the ability to simply jump out and shoot a beautiful B-17, hop back in, and charge on to the next good-looking spot, it really contributed to the end result of be-

ing able to shoot 352 negatives of 60 different planes.

So, after a restless night's sleep, I was at the gate ready to go at 8:00 A.M. This was before the sun was very bright. My first shots of the P-47s, A-24s, and P-40s were actually taken on a tripod in the early-morning light.

My photographic quest had certain guidelines, and each picture had to adhere to the following standards: The first rule was photographing complete airplanes—for engineless aircraft were not tolerated by collectors at that time. In addition, I was taking a number of duplicate negatives for trading purposes. The second goal was to photograph different block numbers, again a fetish that was a result of working with James C. Fahey, enthusiasts of the period, and AAF tech orders. This took some extra time to accomplish because it meant stopping, walking to the nose to read the data legend for the block number, and then going to another and another in search of that elusive difference. Naturally, I was interested in markings and tail letters and attempted to get a sample of each one, but not on incomplete planes. As a result, I did not bother with large areas of B-17s and B-24s where the planes were already being disassembled.

I will never forget the utter frustration of that fateful lunch hour. Can you imagine sitting in the middle of 5,000 airplanes with camera in hand, and unable to do anything about it? It was the guard's lunch hour, so naturally everything stopped. It seemed like one o'clock would never come, but it did and we were off again for another part of the field. Since I was anxious to get as many types as possible, it was necessary to drive over the entire area to see what was available. You must realize that the knowledge of the field from looking at these aerial photos was not available to me at the time, and you cannot see past two rows of planes when you are in the middle of such a forest of aircraft. So when you are on the ground driving, you really don't know what is up ahead.

Late in the afternoon, we got to the B-25s, B-26s, and A-20s. It's interesting now to look at the negatives

This was Larkins' last photo of Kingman, taken at about 250 feet above the ground, depicting just a small fraction of those B-17s that met their fate at Kingman. Of particular interest here are two Fortresses: the unusual all-black B-17 carrying the "triangle-J" tail markings of the 351st Bomb Group and, parked to the left of it, the better-known *A Bit of Lace*. This 447th Bomb Group veteran flew 83 missions over Europe and carried famous nose art inspired by Milton Caniff, a prominent American cartoonist during the 1940s. *A Bit of Lace* has also been featured as the markings for popular B-17 scale model plastic kit. *William T. Larkins*

and see how camera shake began to creep in (even at 1/400th- second exposure) as the time grew shorter. I would judge from the negatives that the A-20s were the last planes shot in a frenzy of activity to get as much as possible before 5:00 P.M.

And of course, that doesn't mean shooting photos up to 5:00 P.M.—it means driving back to the office so that the guard can check out by 5:00 P.M.—a considerable difference in a field that has aircraft stretching for five miles.

The next morning I used what little money I had left to rent a Piper J-3 Cub to shoot aerial photos of the area. That has since turned out to be the most historically valuable of all I did, but I did not realize this at the time. I started photographing at about 1,000 feet above the ground, but by the last photo (the lineup of B-17s showing the all-black Triangle J plane), I had successfully talked the pilot down to about 250 feet for one more pass. Other than one photo in *Life* magazine and a shot in the *Los Angeles Times*, I have never seen another aerial view of Kingman.

I feel that the 13 photos taken on that flight have really been a contribution to aviation history. Their publication many times around the world has formed the mental image that most enthusiasts have of this historic collection.

One of my intentions in sharing these photos with fellow enthusiasts is to correct the mistaken impression that the planes at Kingman were all B-17s. The emphasis on the B-17 in all previously published material has left most people with this idea. I would guess that about one-third of the planes were B-17s, one-third were B-24s, and the other third was made up of a mixture of several types such as the A-20, B-25, and B-26. Jerry McLain, a local journalist, states in his article in *Arizona Highways* magazine (May 1947) that there were Douglas A-26s and Boeing B-29s at Kingman, but I did not see any when I was there. He also describes "hundreds of P-47 Thunderbolts," but I only saw one; and he mentions 678 P-38s compared to about 100 when I was there.

About half of the B-17s and one-third of the B-24s were returned combat aircraft, with the remainder made up of planes from training units in the United States. Some of the B-24s may have been brand-new, for as Alan Blue says in his excellent book *The B-24 Liberator*, there were 400 unused B-24s in storage pools at the end of the war.

The tables (see appendix IV) are provided to give an idea of the combat groups that were represented there as well as the diversity and magnitude of their representation. It is also hoped that they might contain an identity, or serial number, that may help readers with their research, or others with a personal interest in an aircraft that they once flew. My trip to Kingman was the most memorable experience of my lifetime, and one that I think will never happen again

Kingman Aircraft

Photographed by William T. Larkins
on February 7, 1947

*Additional information culled from the Larkins photos
can be found in Appendix IV.

RA-24B-1 -DT	42-54288	B-24M-40-CO	44-42606
TA-20G-40-DO	43-21657	B-25D	FW247
TA-20G-45-DO	43-21756	B-25D-35-N C	43-3666
TA-20H-1-DO	44-23	B-25D-35-NC	FW267
A-20H-10-DO	44-308	TB-25-10-NA	43-4897
TA-20J-15-DO	43-21558	TB-26B-10-MA	41-18214
TA-20J-15-DO	44-21704	TB-26B-35-MA	41-32012
TA-20K-15-DO	44-731	TB-26B-35-MA	41-32033
B-17F-30-DL	42-3182	TB-26B-40-MO	42-43332
B-17G-5-VE	42-39926	TB-26B-40-MO	42-43338
B-17G-15-VE	42-97510	RB-26B-40-MO	42-43347
B-17G-40- BO	42-97123	TB-26C-20-MO	41-35098
B-17G-50-DL	44-6315	TB-26C-21 -MO	41-35153
B-17G-65-DL	44-8627	TB-26C-45-MO	42-107495
B-17G-70-BO	43-37716	B-26G-10-MA	43-34543
B-17G-70-DL	44-6906	B-32-1-CF	42-108480
B-17G-80-VE	44-8745	TB-32-10-CF	42-108500
B-17G-95-DL	43-38738	B-32-20-CF	42-108537
RLB-30	AL594	C-87-2-10	42-6985
RB-24A	40-2369	F-5E-4-LO	44-24560
TB-24J-66-CO	42-100052	RF-6C-10-NT	44-10911
B-24J -205-CO	44-41315	TP-40N-30-CU	44-7068
B-24J-208-CO	44-41331	TP-40N-35-CU	44-7541
RB-24L-11-FO	44-49630	P-40R	41-13659
TB-24L-11 -FO	44-49646	TP-40R	41-13682
B-24M-11-FO	44-50689	P-47D-4-HE	42-22729
B-24M-11-FO	44-50725	RP-63A-6-BE	42-68959
B-24M-11-FO	44-50734	P-63A-6-BE	42-69013
B-24M-16-FO	44-50867	P-63A-9-BE	42-69425
B-24M-31-FO	44-51505	RP-63A-9-BE	42-69501

and none of them actually matched the numbers kept in Washington.

Today, Julian Myers still remembers the inventory circus that went on at Kingman in 1946. "No one ever asked me, but I had papers on every airplane that came on the field," recalled Myers. "One day some WAA officials came in and said, very confidentially behind closed doors, that they wanted the office manager and me to go with them and count the airplanes. I said, 'You're silly. I got them all here in the file.' But no, they wanted us to absolutely count them. So we went out for three or four days counting airplanes. When we finished this fellow said, 'You know, the auditing department has counted these airplanes, and I can't reconcile our count with their count.' I told him that we had traveled east and west in front of the planes and they (the auditors) traveled north and south and walked between them. 'There is only one way to accurately count the planes and that's the way we did it," Myers said. Well, he couldn't seem to get the figures together so he said, 'We've got to count them again.' So, we counted them again, and he finally went off to Washington with the list. I was never so glad to get rid of somebody in my life. This fellow later phoned me, and said, 'Our count doesn't match the military's count.' I told him to take the list and tell all concerned that this is it. Take it or leave it. 'I can't', he said. 'I threw the list away!' I told him that I could give him another count of the airplanes by the day after tomorrow. He said, 'What do you mean?' I confessed to him that I had made a copy of what we had done. Each day after we finished our count I would lock the list in my desk. At night my chief guard would open my desk and make a copy of the things we had done that day and lock them back up. 'So I've got a copy that I can send to you,' I told him. 'Oh my God, please!' he said. After that, I never heard another word about the airplane count."[96]

Satisfied with a final count of 5,483 airplanes, the investigating committee moved on to question why Wunderlich Construction was given the 40 extra aircraft after the original bill of sale document had been issued. (Accounting discrepancies also appeared on the bill of sale documents that were sent to the

Checker tail B-24M-11-FO, serial number 44-50725, has had its nose turret sprayed silver, and wears the nose art of a young lady talking on the telephone. The plane served with the 15th Air Force's 459th Bomb Group. After returning stateside, the unit was inactivated at Sioux Falls Army Air Field on August 28, 1945, and its aircraft flown to storage. *William T. Larkins*

winners of the other four storage depots, but none of these companies bothered to protest the WAA's final count as Wunderlich had. They opted instead to pay a supplementary amount for the extra aircraft they received.) Colonel Carey confirmed that a letter dated February 27, 1947, was initially sent to Martin Wunderlich informing him that he was not entitled to the extra 40 aircraft because the bill of sale was issued for only 5,443 warbirds.[97] He correspondingly said that General Mollison had later reversed the WAA's official position on the bill of sale and awarded the extra 40 planes to Wunderlich. General Mollison's reversal was based on two facts. First, the language used in the WAA sales literature had clearly stated that: "The sealed bid or proposal must contain an offering for the *total* nonflyable aircraft on the particular field to which it refers. Offerings for a portion of the nonflyable aircraft on any field will not be considered."[98] Second, Martin Wunderlich himself made a convincing argument that he had, in fact, used the 5,483 figure from the June 14, 1946, memorandum to formulate his final bid.[99]

In retrospect, one can clearly see the origins of confusion over the sale of surplus aircraft at Kingman's Depot 41. The WAA was trying to efficiently sell the aircraft at the five surplus depots without damaging the country's economy. However, they made the mistake of accepting bids before accurately reconciling the multiple inventories that took place during the months of May and June 1946. General Mollison, and the other WAA officials, didn't really foresee that their actions and mistakes in counting the airplanes would somehow lead to a Senate investigation. In the end, nothing really came of these Senate hearings. The investigating committee didn't produce any evidence to depose the WAA's position on the sale of Kingman's aircraft, nor did they prove that the WAA had favored Wunderlich Construction with inside information. To use Lindsey Youngblood's words: "The whole investigation was a farce."[100]

Few of the 800 people employed by Wunderlich Construction knew of what was going on in Washington, D.C. Every day more airplanes were moved up the process line where a crane would drop a 10-ton steel blade, which measured 10 feet long and 4 inches thick, from a height of approximately 60 feet above each airplane. The weight and the velocity of the cutting device easily sliced through the thin aircraft metal. To the employees at Kingman this was their job, but to many Americans these old obsolete war veterans held more value than the price of aluminum. Jerry McLain reported in his May 1947 *Arizona Highways* magazine article that occasionally an airman would arrive at the gate and ask to see the

The Dragon and His Tail was the last aircraft scrapped at Kingman. *Robert A. Kropp Collection*

Aviation researcher Doug Scroggins inspects one of the B-17 fuel bladders that litter the area outside the current Kingman airport boundaries. A Boeing stamped fuel cap was found a few yards away. Kingman is still in the aircraft storage business more than fifty years after the massive World War II scrapping operations. A trio of ex-Continental Airlines 737s is to the left and a large number of Brasilias are parked in the background to the right. *Nicholas A. Veronico*

fighter or bomber that he had flown during the war.[101] In 1991, former WAA Real Property Manager Fred Nimz recalled an encounter he had with a distraught airman at Kingman. Apparently, this young war veteran was very disturbed that his B-17 was going to be destroyed, so he crawled into the body of the plane with a .45- caliber pistol in his hand. He told Nimz: "This used to be my plane. My commanding officer died when I flew this plane." Nimz talked to the young man for some time, then had a Catholic priest brought to the scene. Eventually, the airman handed over the gun, but before he left the airplane he pulled back some lining next to the pilot seat and showed Nimz and the priest the bloodstains. According to Nimz, Walter Winchell later relayed this touching story to the American public on his radio program.[102]

In the middle of June 1947, Wunderlich Construction applied for and received an extension on its salvage license through April 30, 1948. Sometime in the early spring of 1948, the last of Wunderlich's airplanes were salvaged at Kingman. One of these was the famous B-24 Liberator from the 43rd Bomb Group named *The Dragon and His Tail*.[103] In July 1948, Storage Depot 41 was released to the Mohave County Government to be used as an airport.[104]

Today, some of the old buildings are still actively used at Kingman Airport and, every once in a while, reunions are sponsored to honor the men and women who worked and trained there. Surprisingly, many parts are still scattered across the desert—much to the delight of aviation historians and aviation souvenir hunters. The city of Kingman, Arizona, is also the home of the Mohave Museum of History and Arts, which displays artifacts that chronicle the history of Kingman Army Air Field as well as Storage Depot 41. One of the more interesting pieces in the museum's collection is the nose art taken from a B-17 named *Lucky Partners*. This particular Flying Fortress served in the Eighth Air Force, 477th Bomb Group in England before being salvaged at Kingman.[105] Its nose artwork depicts Walt Disney cartoon characters, Jose (the parrot) and Donald Duck. Sadly, this is the only known nose art to survive the Kingman salvage operation.

CHAPTER 3
Additional Army Air Force Disposal Sites

Nearly 70 airports and former AAF bases were engaged in selling surplus aircraft. (See Appendix I for additional fields.) The majority of the sites sold nontactical aircraft that could be adopted for one civilian use or another, such as cargo or passenger transportation or aerial applications, including fire bombing and insect spraying.

Dashing and accomplished aviator Paul Mantz acquired one field of more than 450 aircraft, and this single transaction has captivated the public ever since. Mantz bought Searcy Field, which is located approximately one mile northwest of the town of Stillwater in the north central part of Oklahoma. The airfield was established as the Stillwater Municipal Airport in 1929 but was renamed after its first manager, George Searcy, was killed in an airplane crash shortly afterward. The airfield remained as a grass strip through 1943, but was improved in 1936 when the federal Works Progress Administration built a large rock hangar for airfield use. A local barnstormer, Al Guthrie, began management of the airport in 1936 and established a flight school that later became part of the federal Civilian Pilot Training Program (CPTP) as the nation began training pilots for the impending war.

In February 1943, the federal government agreed to develop the airport in return for its military use during the war. The CAA's airport improvement program built three new 5,000-foot concrete runways with accompanying taxiways and tarmacs. The Navy assumed control of the airport and designated Searcy Field as an Outlying Field for NAS Clinton, Oklahoma.[106] There is no indication that the Navy used the airfield for anything other than a transient training field. Meanwhile, the CPTP activities were moved to a new grass strip located south of the airport and designated Stillwater No. 2.

At the end of May 1945, the Navy transferred the field to the RFC for use as a storage depot.[107] The first surplus aircraft, a flight of four P-47s, arrived at the airport on June 22, 1945, and within two months nearly 500 surplus aircraft had been placed into storage.[108] This number included 228 Consolidated B-24

A rare color photo of veteran B-24s parked at Albuquerque, New Mexico. The area that contained the scrapyard is not on the present-day Kirtland AFB; rather, it was located at Oxnard Field, a dirt strip located several miles east of the current base. *Kirtland AFB Historian's Office*

When Bernard Schulte arrived at Bush Field, Augusta, Georgia, to purchase an AT-6, he spent a few moments capturing the aircraft on film. The P-64 was built by North American for the Peruvian and Thai Air Forces. Only 13 were built and the Thai aircraft were requisitioned by the AAF as high-performance trainers, 41-18087 being the last aircraft of its type built. *Bernard Schulte*

The Curtiss SNC Falcon was the Navy's version of the CW.22 two-seat advanced trainer, and was powered by a 420-horsepower R-975. The Navy bought 300 Falcons. This unidentified example is slowly sinking into the Georgia soil. *Bernard Schulte*

variants, of which 82 were Navy PB4Y-1s (see Table 1). Of particular note is that many of the secret Carpetbagger B-24s, used covertly in the European Theater of Operations (ETO) and distinctive for their all-black paint schemes, were stored at the airfield.

Additionally, a large number of bombers stored at Searcy were distinguished combat veterans. Among the B-17s were *Hell's Angels* (48 missions), *Knock Out Dropper* (75 missions), and *Ruthie II*. The B-24s included Pacific veteran *Hellzaoppin* and the ETO's *Pappy Yokum*. Many of these aircraft had been relegated to stateside training units after their combat tours and requisite war bond rallies. As such, they were among the first tactical aircraft declared surplus and thus were directed to one of the first large depots established by the RFC.

Initial efforts were made to "pickle" the aircraft but, with the high rate of arrival that was occurring during July and August 1945, that effort soon gave way to just segregating the aircraft by type and parking them in long rows in anticipation of eventual scrapping.

After August 1945, the field's inventory stabilized at about 475 tactical aircraft. This number included 306 four-engine bombers, 34 twin-engine bombers, and 135 single-engine fighters. There is no record of any civil sales of these aircraft for flying purposes between the establishment of the depot until February 1946 when the lot was sold.

However, there was plenty of local evidence that "liberated" parts of the aircraft did find their way into local farms and households. One Stillwater ranch supply store recently discovered that a long-held mechanism used to stretch new rope consisted of a B-24 bomb bay door hydraulic actuator and tank and a P-47 landing gear extension handle, all of which came from aircraft stored at Searcy Field. Numerous radios, instruments, and other components have also surfaced over the years.

Surplus aircraft on the ramp in late 1945 or early 1946, at Searcy Field, Oklahoma. These four aircraft—an F6F Hellcat, a North American AT-6, a B-25 Mitchell, and a P-51 Mustang—were transferred to Oklahoma State University for educational purposes. The rows of surplus aircraft in the background, however, were those sold to Hollywood pilot Paul Mantz in February 1946. The hangar in the center of the photo is still on the field. The fate of the four aircraft transferred is unknown, though rumors suggest the Mustang eventually ended up with the Israeli Air Force. *Stillwater Airport Memorial Museum*

The Stillwater Airport Memorial Museum

The Stillwater Airport Memorial Museum, established in 1992 by a small group of Oklahoma aviation enthusiasts, has documented much of the history of Searcy Field. The museum began as a glass display case located in the airport terminal, and now occupies a jam-packed display room with dozens of historical photographs, displays, artifacts, and memorabilia.

Although the museum's chronicle of Oklahoma aviation begins in the early 1920s, there is no doubt that the emphasis is upon those warplanes that made their last landing at Stillwater. Three large display tables contain bits and pieces of Boeing B-17s, Consolidated B-24s and PB4Ys, Curtiss P-40s, Republic P-47s, and North American B-25s. All of the airplane parts on display have been recovered from surrounding fields.

Carefully lined up and numbered, each piece holds clues to its own story. Pick up a rectangular access plate and rub your fingers across it. Notice that the aluminum part has faded black paint over olive drab: this is a part from a famous B-24 Carpetbagger, the secret group that flew nighttime intruder missions over Nazi-occupied Europe to insert agents and do other mischief. The factory-applied olive drab camouflage was oversprayed with flat black paint by an Eighth Air Force depot for the nighttime raids, and the Carpetbaggers were among the only "Mighty Eighth" bombers so painted. This finish differs from an identically shaped access plate lying beside it, which is from a Navy PB4Y-1 patrol bomber, if the Navy blue paint is any indicator. Next to these parts lies a small control panel from the bombardier's station

Among the artifacts collected by the Stillwater Airport Memorial Museum is this pair of B-24 vertical stabilizers. Evidently they were removed from B-24s parked on the field in 1946, and used as billboards to advertise a local auto-body shop. They were eventually hauled away and stored on a local farm. The museum was able to recover the parts for future display. The identity of the aircraft they came from is not yet known. There are no apparent identification markings on either stabilizer but repaired combat damage is evident.
Scott A. Thompson

in a B-17, toggle switches worn from either countless fingers or years in the dirt, or both. Perhaps this long-lost panel endured a baptism of fire over Schweinfurt in October 1943; nobody will ever know.

When the fighters and bombers arrived at Stillwater during the summer and fall of 1945, they first lined the runways and taxiways in a random order of dispersal. Later, they were pulled and taxied into somewhat orderly rows segregated by type. After the warplanes were sold to Paul Mantz, crews began working their way up and down the lines disassembling them. In the process of stripping the aircraft, numerous small parts were dropped and left, particularly plates removed to gain access to airplane structures. As the museum staff has explored the fields, personalities of the airplane scrappers have emerged. Some crews were neat, carefully removing screws from panels and grouping small parts together in little piles. Other crews literally ripped aluminum panels off the airplanes to get to the structure, and left any pieces where they fell. Some major assemblies were unbolted, but in many cases they were simply cut apart with welding torches. Today, little chunks of aluminum slag can be found in places where molten metal dripped from the airplanes.

One nearby field that held several dozen B-24s still has some deep tire ruts where B-24s were dragged into rows for storage. Obviously the ground was soggy that day in 1945, for a careful observer can follow individual tracks to a B-24's final spot. Trees and bushes are now sprouting up in the unused field and it won't be long before the field will be reclaimed completely by nature, leaving the deep ruts as a curious monument to an obscure day.

Out in the museum storage hangar is a pair of huge, slab-sided B-24 vertical stabilizers. These bear the scars of combat: aluminum patches cover hard-earned flak or bullet wounds suffered somewhere in the distant past. A local auto-body shop proprietor acquired the Liberator parts in 1946 and placed them along the main highway at each end of town, painted as billboards to advertise his business. Years later, someone thought they were eyesores, and they ended up lying in a pasture next to a farmer's barn. The museum learned the farmer was selling them as scrap and purchased them for eight cents per pound. Detective work has yet to uncover any combat or identification markings that may still exist below layers of advertising paint.

The museum volunteers, led by Museum Director Woody Harris, have amassed a large collection of technical orders and manuals for each of the various types of airplanes scrapped on the field. These are used to trace part numbers that help identify or verify the heritage of some of the less obvious components. Harris was instrumental in the establishment of the museum. He spent the better part of 30 years running the audio-visual department for Oklahoma State University. One day, after he had retired, he was visiting one of the campus departments and discovered boxes of old unwanted negatives that were slated for disposal by the university. Looking through a few of them, he found aerial photos of Searcy Field showing hundreds of parked fighters and bombers. Harris had heard of the scrapping operation that occurred at Stillwater but had never seen any photographs of the activity. Realizing the treasure trove he had stumbled upon, he saved the negatives and eventually returned all the nonaviation negatives to the university for its archives. The aviation material, however, now resides with the museum collection.

The curator of the museum is aviation historian and author John Dienst. Aside from contributing to the ongoing historical and archeological activities of the museum, Dienst has spent much of the past few years researching the history of each of the 475 aircraft that came to Searcy Field. For those aircraft used in combat, each airplane has a story waiting to be told. Combat veterans and veterans groups are now contacting Dienst and the museum staff with increasing regularity as news of the museum and those aircraft that ended up at Searcy spreads. Dienst is assembling this vast research project into a book that, when published, will bring all the stories and photographs together in one place. It should be a fitting tribute to the men and machines forever tied to those mysterious tire ruts marking the grassy pastures surrounding the Stillwater Airport.

An aerial view of aircraft parked at Searcy Field near Stillwater, Oklahoma, in 1946. The airport, which was used by the Navy during the war, eventually held 475 aircraft and was the first large-scale sale of surplus airplanes held by the RFC. Almost all of these aircraft were disassembled and the parts shipped out for smelting at St. Louis, Missouri, during 1946 and 1947. *Stillwater Airport Memorial Museum*

The aircraft remained stored at Searcy Field through the balance of 1945. Then, on February 19, 1946, nationally known aviator Paul Mantz purchased the 475 tactical aircraft stored at Searcy Field for $55,425.68, or approximately $117 per aircraft. One can only speculate how Mantz—who had served as an Air Corps major during wartime service, was well connected in the aviation and entertainment industry, and was by all accounts a very shrewd businessman—was able to conclude such a lucrative deal. There are no surviving individuals or records that might shed light on the arrangement. In any event, this became the first field-size sale concluded by the WAC, which had supplanted the RFC on January 1, 1946. The sale was actually part of a test program to determine the most efficient method of aircraft disposal: field-size sale to contractors; scrapping by government agencies and subsequent sale of scrap to

smelters; or government smelting of aircraft and subsequent sale of aluminum ingots.[109]

Peculiar to the deal negotiated between Mantz and the WAC was the lack of a "scrap only" provision. This provision was prominent in agreements made between the WAA, which supplanted the WAC in March 1946, and scrapping contractors five months later. The Mantz agreement contains no restrictions to the subsequent use of the 475 aircraft, although there is a reference in the contract that it was "further subject to the terms and conditions of a certain agreement," which was never recorded and the terms of which remain unknown today.[110] That Mantz utilized some of his new airplanes in such well-publicized and highly visible enterprises as movie making and air racing would also suggest that there was no "scrap only" provision in the contract.

Although the B-18 was obsolete at the beginning of the war, many flew anti-submarine missions off the East and Gulf Coasts of the United States. By mid-1944 most had been relegated to the role of trainer. Under the B-18's right wing are a number of Budd RB-1 Conestogas, a twin-engine transport built using stainless steel. Only 17 were delivered to the Navy, and the remaining 183 on the contract were canceled. The Conestogas had a high wing and a rear-loading cargo ramp. An AAF order for 600—to be delivered as C-93s—was also canceled when the war ended. Of the canceled aircraft, 9 were completed and delivered to Flying Tiger Airlines for cargo work. *Bernard Schulte*

On the same day Mantz purchased the aircraft from the WAC, he also entered into a partnership agreement with two individuals, J. W. Heath and L. B. Hapgood, to form the Heath-Hapgood-Mantz partnership. Heath and Hapgood evidently contributed $70,000 to get into the partnership, while Mantz contributed 464 of his 475 aircraft.[111] Contrary to other published accounts, it is clear from the record that Mantz at the earliest point decided to draw only 11 aircraft, consisting of one B-17, one B-24, one A-20, one B-25, two P-51s, three P-40s, one P-47, and one P-39, for his own personal use. The remainder of the aircraft were to be scrapped or otherwise sold by the partnership for maximum profit.

Later accounts indicate that Mantz bragged that he had sold the gasoline in the airplanes for more than his $55,000 investment; certainly he made $15,000 from his partnership arrangement before any airplane scrap was sold.[112] He put his small fleet of 11 surplus airplanes into use: the two P-51Cs became

Aircraft Sold at Searcy Field, Stillwater, Oklahoma, February 1946	
Type	Number
A-20	1
A-36	1
AT-23	7
B-17	78
B-18	1
B-24	144
B-25	10
B-26	15
F-7	2
P-39	6
P-40	90
P-47	31
P-51	7
PB4Y-1	82
Total	473

Culver's PQ-14 manned aerial target certainly stands out among the greenery of Bush Field in its red/orange paint scheme. More than 1,400 were built. *Bernard Schulte*

his blood-red brace of air racers for the postwar Bendix races, while his B-25H was rebuilt as a custom cameraship. The B-17 was used in several films, as were the P-40s. The B-24, however, disappeared from sight and its fate remains unknown.

For the 464 aircraft entered into the partnership agreement, fate was more certain. Unlike other postwar scrapping operations, there was no smelter used at Searcy Field. Instead, each of the airframes was disassembled on location into manageable parts that could be loaded onto large trucks. The trucks then were driven across town to the railroad depot where the scrap was loaded onto railcars for transport to St. Louis. Once there, the Leonard Metal Works scrap metal company reduced the airplane parts to aluminum and iron ingots.

From the record, it would seem that the process was messy and disorganized. In late 1946, the city of Stillwater was complaining to the Navy (still the leaseholder) and the WAA about the condition of the airfield and requesting a concerted effort to finish the scrapping and return the field to the city.[113] However, local residents recall that at least one B-24 was still on the field as late as 1949 (Mantz's elusive

Liberator), and as much as a quarter-century later there were still eight substantial piles of scrap residue around the airfield. One local resident, Tim Fitzgerald, recalls that as a boy in the early 1970s he used a Sperry ball turret frame from one of the scrap piles and some rope to make a swing. He and his friends routinely used airplane Plexiglas for target shooting with BB guns, and recalls that the scrap piles contained fuel caps, data plates, armored glass, and other small airframe parts.

It is also apparent that some of the tactical aircraft did make it out from Searcy in a more covert fashion. Mantz's remaining six P-51Cs were reported as disassembled and the parts sold to several dealers. These parts were subsequently reassembled, and several were used as air racers and a number were covertly exported overseas, as was a B-25H.

Today, there remains much evidence of the storage and disassembly process that occurred at Stillwater. Walking over any of the grassy fields surrounding the runways and taxiways reveals small aircraft parts: aluminum plates removed from wings to gain access to wing bolts, riveted panels, Plexiglas pieces, small tubes and actuators, propeller hub parts, and the like. The Stillwater Airport Memorial Association (see Stillwater Airport Memorial Museum Sidebar) has created a substantial museum with an ever-growing collection of parts, photos, and records of the history of those aircraft once held at Searcy Field. The museum is also conducting ongoing excavations of one-time drainage ditches filled in with small parts and then buried by the aircraft scrappers.

Walnut Ridge Army Air Field, Walnut Ridge, Arkansas

Walnut Ridge Army Air Field, which is located in the northeastern corner of the state of Arkansas, was used during World War II to train Aviation Cadets in the art of basic flying. In mid-1945, the facility was turned over to the Navy, which also used the base to train Naval aviators until shortly after the victory over Japan. At that time the airfield was again put under the control of the AAF. The surplus aircraft were initially brought to Walnut Ridge to be stored for future use. Many of these were flown straight off the assembly line to the so-called boneyard. Reportedly, more than 11,000 warbirds were stored at Walnut Ridge at one time or another.[114] In the fall of 1945, all of the aircraft on the field were officially declared surplus.

What happened at Walnut Ridge, in regards to aircraft disposal, is similar to what transpired at the other WAA depots at that time. Namely, complete airworthy ships were offered for sale to the public, and anyone with the asking price could purchase the World War II airplane of their choice. The WAA's plan was to get rid of the unwanted aircraft as fast as they could, so the pricing was structured in a way that a complete airplane was cheaper than any single component. Airline officials, race pilots, farmers, and the like came to the spacious field to take advantage of the bargain airplanes. Even aircraft manufacturers

This unidentified P-40 waits its turn in line for the smelter. What is unusual about the aircraft is that it wears five German and one Italian kill marks. Most likely, these were applied for a stateside war bond tour. *Grantham Collection*

Actor Dana Andrews walks among the rows of stripped B-17s at the fictionalized "Boone City" depot in the 1946 Academy Award–winning film *The Best Years of Our Lives*. The scene was actually shot at Cal-Aero as the dramatic conclusion to the film. The character played by Andrews, a down-on-his-luck 8th Air Force veteran, finally comes to terms with his peacetime adjustment as he gets a job smashing old airplanes into things for the future, a sentiment echoed by the nation in the early postwar years. *James H. Farmer Collection*

such as Beechcraft got into the act, because it was cheaper to purchase complete, low-time Consolidated Vultee BT-13s than to buy new replacement R-985 engines directly from Pratt & Whitney.[115]

In early 1946, Walnut Ridge also had the distinction of being one of the few WAA depots that had D-model North American P-51 Mustangs for sale. Surplus P-51D Mustangs were somewhat rare in the near-postwar era. The North American fighter was still in active military service, so the numbers of excess P-51s in 1945–1946 were relatively small as compared to the P-38 or P-40. Naturally, the best all-around fighting airplane of World War II was in great

demand and, at $3,500 a copy, garnished the highest selling price of any of its contemporaries.[116] Sales of the Mustangs, however, had to be suspended in early 1946 after the British complained to the U.S. government. Apparently, Rolls-Royce did not want its Merlin engine technology released to the civilian sector, so on March 1, 1946, sale of all variants of the P-51 were halted.[117] But that didn't stop Steve Beville from getting his Mustang.

Beville served as a ferry pilot during the war and flew just about every airplane in the Allied inventory. In early 1946, it was announced that the city of Cleveland, Ohio, would once again host the National

Air Races in September. Beville and his partner, Bruce Raymond, had always wanted to compete in the air races, so they decided to buy a P-51 at their earliest opportunity. At that time, Beville had not yet separated from the AAF and was still ferrying aircraft across the country. On a stop in Washington in late February, Beville went to the WAA office and requested a P-51. WAA officials were more than happy to oblige but they told him that he had better hurry up and get down to Walnut Ridge because sale of Mustangs was scheduled to stop the following month. There was no way that Beville could get to Arkansas in time, so a deal was made with the WAA that allowed him and Raymond to buy a Mustang after the March deadline. Their P-51D-15-NA, AAF serial number 44-15651, ended up being the last aircraft of its type to be sold from Walnut Ridge.[118]

Although aircraft sales were going fairly well, they still weren't producing the desired results for the WAA. The bottom line indicated that the WAA wasn't bringing in enough money from aircraft sales to cover the expenses of keeping places like Walnut Ridge open. So a plan was derived to suspend all aircraft sales and auction off the entire holdings of some of their larger surplus depots located at Kingman, Arizona; Clinton, Oklahoma; Albuquerque, New Mexico; and Ontario, California. In July 1946, the TREC of Houston, Texas, submitted a bid of $1,817,738 and won the opportunity to salvage the 4,821 airplanes stored at Walnut Ridge.[119] An approximate breakdown of their award went as follows:

Reconnaissance	26
Fighters	1,115
Light Bombers	48
Medium Bombers	809
Heavy Bombers	2,774
Advanced Trainers	49

Prior to bidding, executives from TREC applied their construction background and developed simple and efficient salvage processes. They studied every type of aircraft at Walnut Ridge and calculated the time and cost of breaking down an airplane to its simplest elements.[120] As a result, TREC was highly

The award for efficient use of space goes to the scrapppers at Walnut Ridge. The unusual storage methods did produce a number of interesting photographs, including this shot of 14 engineless P-40s. *National Archives*

organized and ready to start its salvage operation when the WAA issued the bill of sale for the aircraft at Walnut Ridge in September 1946. The WAA's count of the aircraft at their Walnut Ridge facility was in error by approximately 50 aircraft. In contrast to what happened at Kingman, TREC didn't dispute the government's final inventory figures, nor did they protest the language used in the WAA sales literature. TREC simply paid the WAA $21,060.19 for the extra aircraft.[121] After being awarded the airplanes on the field, TREC allied with the high bidders that won surplus aircraft at the other four fields to form a single company to oversee the overall salvage operations at Kingman, Clinton, Albuquerque, Ontario and, of course, Walnut Ridge. Three men, Slim Dahlstrum, J. E. Walters, and George Darneille, all of whom were associates of the Brown brothers, ran the newly established ACC.[122]

Soon to be scrapped, the engineless XB-24N, serial number 44-48753, awaits the end at Patterson Field in January 1946. *William T. Larkins*

By contract, TREC/ACC were not allowed to sell complete flyable aircraft from Walnut Ridge. The WAA was concerned that the winners of the surplus airplanes might venture into the used aircraft sales business, so provisions were outlined in the salvage license to forbid such practices, but a few warplanes did manage to legally escape into civil aircraft registry.

In the summer of 1947, J. D. Reed, a well-known Beechcraft dealer from Houston, Texas, and William P. Odom, future around-the-world speed record holder, were both independently looking for an airplane that could be used to compete in the 1947 Bendix Trophy Race. Reed was interested in acquiring a Lockheed P-38 Lightning, while Odom fancied the very fast Republic P-47M. Republic Aviation told Odom that all but one of their P-47Ms had been sent to Europe before VE day, and they were subsequently scrapped overseas. He was also told that the sole surviving P-47M (actually YP-47M-1-RE) ended up at Walnut Ridge.[123]

Meanwhile, Reed wasn't looking for just any P-38. He wanted an early, more streamlined version of the famed Lightning. Most of the older P-38s were among the first aircraft to be surplused after the war and all ended up on the five fields (including Walnut Ridge) that were auctioned by the WAA in 1946. The airplanes that were desired by Odom and Reed were to be found at Walnut Ridge, but TREC wasn't allowed to sell any flyable aircraft. Reed found a way around the government restrictions by offering to trade a P-38L (AAF serial number 44-27086) that he had earlier purchased from the WAA to TREC in exchange for a P-38F (AAF serial number 43-2181).[124] George Darneille didn't really have a problem with the trade but took the precaution of contacting the Office of Aircraft Disposal in Washington, D.C. In a telegram he wrote that the purpose of the trade was to afford a better aircraft to an individual who had previously purchased a flyable aircraft. Darneille's telegram also made it very clear that TREC would not gain any financial benefit from the trade.[125]

The WAA approved the trade, and J. D. Reed sent one of his pilots, Ivis Hill, to Walnut Ridge to complete the transaction. Bill Odom didn't have to jump through the same legal hoops, because his dream P-47M had already been dismantled by TREC. Odom merely wrote a $2,000 check for miscellaneous P-47 parts with a Pratt & Whitney R2800 engine and trucked his purchase off the field.[126] Both the Reed

Row upon row of Martin B-26 Marauders at Cal-Aero, some parked with consecutive serial numbers, on May 22, 1946. *William T. Larkins*

P-38F and Odom P-47M would later enter the 1947 Bendix Trophy Race. Odom's Thunderbolt developed a massive fuel leak the morning of the race and there wasn't enough time to fix the problem before the start. The P-38F would suffer a more drastic fate. Reed sold his new Lightning to his good friend Glen McCarthy not long after Hill returned with the fighter from Walnut Ridge. McCarthy sent the airplane to the Aviation Maintenance Corporation in Van Nuys, California, which basically converted the former fighter into a flying gas tank. Unfortunately, pilot James Ruble would lose the right tip tank while taking off in the Bendix race. Later an engine/turbo fire forced Ruble to abandon the race plane over Arizona.

TREC won additional contracts during its stay at Walnut Ridge, supplying the Air Force with spare parts.

One of the most unique aircraft at Cal-Aero Field was 43-47419, the last of 17 C-46Es built. The contract called for 550 aircraft, but the war cut production short. The "E" model differed from other C-46s in its stepped windshield and three, rather than four, blade propellers. This aircraft was destined for the Nationalist Chinese Air Force, but stopped short of its delivery destination on the West Coast. *William T. Larkins*

Unlike all of the other AAF storage fields, Cal-Aero had a number of Navy aircraft including a PBY, and several Grumman J2F amphibians. This TBF-1 photo is an important historical record of the Navy aircraft at Cal-Aero, but of real interest to aviation historians is the rare Northrop P-61 Black Widow night fighter in the background. *John Mitchell via Larkins*

The value of these contracts amounted to more than $3.5 million, which exceeded the original purchase price of the aircraft at Walnut Ridge by a factor of two.[127] As one might expect, TREC was in a position to gouge the government for the critical parts needed by the Air Force; however, the parent company, Brown and Root Construction, wasn't really interested in making excessive profits on aircraft component sales because its focus was on aluminum.[128] For example: in 1947 the Strategic Air Force discovered that the Hamilton Standard propellers on their B-29s wouldn't operate properly in extremely cold weather. As a quick fix, the Air Force decided to replace the failing propellers with Curtiss-Wright electric types that had been employed on the Consolidated B-32. Curtiss-Wright had long stopped manufacturing B-32 propellers, and all of the Dominators had been sold surplus at either Kingman, Arizona, or Walnut Ridge, Arkansas. Purchasing Agent and Contracting Officer Nate Silverston, at Wright Field, contacted TREC and asked if they could supply 300 sets of B-32-type propellers. TREC

immediately stopped salvaging B-32s and sold the Air Force the required blades, converters, and all the other necessary equipment for $16,500 ($55 per propeller).[129] Silverston figured that it would have taken Curtis-Wright two years to produce the propellers and would have cost more than $2 million if the Air Force had bought them new.[130]

Later, Silverston contacted TREC about B-25 propellers. They came back with a price of $75 each. Silverston inquired about the price difference between the two types of propellers and TREC responded with the following: "The B-32 propeller is made out of metal which is not aluminum. We are interested in aluminum. The B-25 propeller is an aluminum propeller. For that reason the salvage value of the B-25 propeller is more, and we are therefore charging you $75 instead of $55."[131]

The fuel, oil, and other fluids in the Walnut Ridge aircraft didn't seem to attract as much attention as they had at Kingman. It has been reported that all multi-engine aircraft were required to stop in St. Louis and refuel before landing at Walnut

An interesting aerial view taken at Cal-Aero Field in 1946 showing to good advantage the rows of aircraft parked on the west end of the airport. This field is now known as Chino Airport and it has become a national center of warbird restoration and operation. The four big hangars in the middle of the photo still exist, and the buildings behind the two center hangars were used as the exterior set for the television series *Twelve O'Clock High* filmed at Chino in the mid-1960s. *William T. Larkins*

Ridge.[132] It is difficult to determine, some 55 years later, how long this practice of refueling surplus aircraft prior to being mothballed at Walnut Ridge continued. It is likely that such refueling stops were ordered during the early days because the RFC/WAA, acting as an agent for the AAF, were pickling approximately 10 percent of the best, low-time aircraft just in case they were quickly needed for some other conflict. However, it is just as likely that practice of storing obsolete aircraft with full fuel tanks was discontinued over time.

TREC and ACC completed their salvage operation at Walnut Ridge in late 1947, but this wasn't the end for either company. TREC and ACC moved on to salvage the aircraft stored at Altus Field, Oklahoma. TREC and ACC also continued to sell aircraft components and, in some cases, complete aircraft back the U.S. Air Force through the Korean War.

Cal-Aero Field, Ontario, California

Cal-Aero Field, located in Ontario, California, was the smallest of the five aircraft storage facilities auctioned off by the WAA in June 1946. Sharp and Fellows Contracting Company of Los Angeles joined the ranks of four other construction firms that successfully submitted winning bids for a piece of approximately 20,000 surplus aircraft the WAA offered for sale. Sharp and Fellows' $404,593 tender outdistanced other companies that bid on the 1,340 warplanes parked at Cal-Aero.[133]

Many aviation historians have long believed that George and Herman Brown, founders of Brown and Root Construction of Houston, Texas, formed a coalition of five construction companies to individually bid on the surplus aircraft.[134] These five companies carefully thought through the bidding process and put together offers that effectively cornered the postwar

America and its allies won the war because they were able to equip their forces with outstanding weapons. The sheer number of Allied aircraft overwhelmed the enemy in both Europe and the Pacific. Miles of factory-fresh P-51Ds were stored at San Antonio after the war. *National Archives*

surplus aircraft business in one clean sweep. But why would construction companies that are more accustomed to building bridges and airfields be interested in getting into the scrapping business? Lindsey S. Youngblood, who worked for both Wunderlich Construction and the TREC, has one possible answer: "The big construction companies found themselves without large projects to bid on due to the cessation of the war. They had cadres of key employees and plenty of equipment standing idle, and the experience to handle large operations."[135] Looking back at the salvaging operations that took place at Cal-Aero and the like during the late 1940s, it appears that the task performed at these fields had more in common with production jobs than with scrapping. With that in mind, a construction company was probably a better fit for the chore of turning combat aircraft into usable goods.

Sharp and Fellows, like the other four winners, participated in the formation of the ACC. The ACC brought in the required experts to build the smelters and develop an efficient salvaging process. The operation at Cal-Aero Field got under way in fall of 1946, and it took less than a year to complete the aircraft

reclamation process. Along the way, renowned director William Wyler used Cal-Aero Field as a location for his Academy Award–winning movie, *The Best Years of Our Lives*. The backdrop of surplus aircraft played well in describing the postwar era of jet propulsion and atomic power and the effect it had on the men who were returning from the war.

It is hard to figure the tonnage of aluminum and other materials salvaged from Cal-Aero aircraft. However, ACC reportedly recovered over 200 million pounds of aluminum, 1,000 ounces of platinum, and 80,000 ounces of silver from the 20,000-plus aircraft that were scrapped in the years immediately following World War II.[136] It is also interesting to note that the gamble that companies such as Sharp and Fellows took in bidding on the surplus business really paid off. At the start of the project, aluminum was running 5 cents a pound, but the high demand in the postwar world soon drove the price up to 22 cents a pound.[137] This earned Sharp and Fellows, along with their other four partners, approximately $40 million, which is not a bad return on the total investment of $6,582,156 that the five companies paid for surplus combat planes.[138]

Today, Cal-Aero Field, a.k.a. Chino Airport, is the mecca of warbirds in the United States. It is the home of The Air Museum–Planes of Fame and Yanks Air Museum. Both of these institutions have on display World War II aircraft that were once saved from the fate of being melted down for the price of aluminum.

Kirtland Army Air Field (Oxnard Field), Albuquerque, New Mexico

What is today Kirtland AFB actually began as two early civil airfields established near Albuquerque, New Mexico. The oldest field was a private airport, Oxnard Field, that was operated beginning in the late 1920s. In 1939 the city of Albuquerque built a municipal airport several miles to the west of Oxnard Field. The Army Air Corps established the Albuquerque Army Air Field on April 5, 1941, on leased land adjacent to the municipal airport. Construction of Albuquerque Army Air Field included improvements to the runways shared with the municipal airport. The field was built as a Works Progress Administration project. The first military aircraft assigned to the field was a Douglas B-18 Bolo that arrived on April 1, 1941. One of the first units assigned to the field was the 19th Bomb Group, based at Albuquerque between June and October 1941 with its B-17Cs and B-17Ds. The field was renamed the Kirtland Army Air Field in February 1942 after the death of a distinguished Army Air Corps pilot, Colonel Roy Kirtland, in May 1941. Beginning in early 1942, Kirtland Army Air Field was under the command of the West Coast Air Corps Training Center and conducted advanced training, a four-engine school, and navigator/bombardier training.[139]

Oxnard Field, located several miles to the east of Kirtland Army Air Field, was adjacent to a small Army Air Depot Training Station for aircraft mechanics. Part of this facility had originally been constructed in the mid-1930s as the Sandia Girls School. After the Army terminated its training depot activities, the War Department established a military hospital on the site and the facility became known generally as the Sandia Base. Some of the old training depot buildings were also used for research work

Alluring *Home Breaker* sits with other B-24s at Albuquerque awaiting the scrapper's torch. *Kirtland AFB Historian's Office*

by the Navy in the development of a proximity fuse for aerial weapons.[140] The Sandia Base and Kirtland AAF, still located several miles apart on a west-east line, remained as separate facilities but both were playing an increasingly large support role in the development of special weapons, including atomic research, under way at the nearby Los Alamos Laboratory. The original Oxnard Field evidently remained intact adjacent to the Sandia Base but was undeveloped with only unpaved runways, a concrete ramp, and several hangars. Oxnard Field was retained under military control, for at some time late in the war the field was placed under the jurisdiction of the AAF Air Technical Service Command and designated for aircraft storage.

In 1945 war-weary fighters and bombers began arriving for storage using the unpaved runways of Oxnard Field. Aircraft stored on the field included B-17s, B-24s, AT-6s, P-38s, P-51s, B-26s, P-39s, and, photos would suggest, at least one Curtiss A-25 Shrike (Helldiver). In the fall of 1945, the airfield was released by the AAF to the RFC for disposal.

This hideous tiger-faced B-24 with fangs and large tongue was certainly the most decorated of the aircraft at Albuquerque. Notice that the markings continue onto the nose turret and the single bomb showing 63 missions. *Kirtland AFB Historian's Office*

Wild Bill, the tommy gun-toting angel, sits at Albuquerque where more than 1,500 aircraft, primarily fighters and bombers, were stored on the airfield. The Compressed Steel Corporation was the high bidder in the July 1946 auction, and they eventually scrapped the airplanes. *Kirtland AFB Historian's Office*

The May 1946 listing published by the RFC listed a total of 1,551 tactical aircraft, including 929 fighters (including some AT-6s), 35 medium bombers, and 567 heavy bombers. It was the fourth largest of the five fields offered in the July auction.

The Compressed Steel Corporation was the successful bidder in the July 1, 1946, auction. The record suggests that Compressed Steel became a partner in ACC to minimize the cost of breaking down the aircraft. However, while some of the other airfields, notably Kingman and Walnut Ridge, had examples of new or nearly new aircraft in the airfield inventory, it appears that all of the aircraft at Oxnard Field were well-worn combat aircraft. There is no indication that usable parts were drawn from aircraft stored at Albuquerque, nor is there any record of these aircraft being sold into the civil market. Evidently, all 1,551 warplanes were scrapped and smelted on the spot.

In July 1945, most of the Sandia Base was turned over to the Army Corps of Engineers for development

This P-39 was probably flown as an aerial gunnery target based on its unusual color scheme. This Airacobra was scrapped at Albuquerque. *Kirtland AFB Historian's Office*

It was somewhat unusual for the RFC to group advanced trainers together with tactical aircraft as their sales were handled differently. Nonetheless, this view shows a field of North American AT-6 Texans parked at Oxnard Field as they awaited scrapping. *Kirtland AFB Historian's Office*

first Eighth Air Force bomber to complete 25 missions and then return stateside. After its obligatory war bond tour, the "Belle" completed its tour of duty as a trainer at McDill Field, Florida. After the war ended, the B-17F was ungratefully sent to Altus for disposal. A chance encounter saved the "Belle" from scrapping. The city of Memphis was able to obtain the aircraft for display purposes and it was flown out in July 1946.

Also, because there was a large number of virtually new Flying Fortresses in storage at Altus, the airfield became the source of many B-17s sold to civil owners between 1946 and 1948. The French *Institut Geographique National* obtained four new B-17s in 1947 for use in international survey work, and several other surplus B-17s were sold to U.S. civil operators—including Transcontinental and Western Airlines (TWA), before the airfield was sold as a lot in May 1947.

In late April 1947, the WAA announced "Another Big Sale" of surplus aircraft in national advertisements.[146] The ads were not specific in either location or terms of sale, no doubt in deference to the problems created in the May 1946 announcement, but included those stored aircraft remaining at Altus. On May 12, 1947, the bids were opened by the WAA, and the Esperado Mining Company of Walnut Ridge, Arkansas, won the award.

Details are sketchy as to how many aircraft were actually sold to Esperado. However, records do indicate that Esperado purchased Lot 3 of the bid sale, which included 423 aircraft and this is presumed to have been the total number of aircraft remaining at Altus in May 1947.[147] Esperado was tied closely, and probably owned outright by, the TREC, the earlier successful bidder for the 4,800 aircraft located at Walnut Ridge. One of TREC's managers was George Darnielle, who signed paperwork in the name of both the Esperado Mining Company and TREC.

Even after the sale for scrapping, those new B-17s at Altus continued to be a source for civil buyers. The WAA terms specified that the aircraft were for salvage and scrapping only, but provided that examples could be sold if any profit beyond the scrap value of the aircraft was returned to the U.S. government. Thus, at least four B-17s were sold by Esperado after May 1947, and in each case Esperado was to pay the U.S. government $2,700 to release the scrap restrictions.[148]

The U.S. Navy also came calling in November 1947, with the intent of purchasing 50 of the 52 B-17s on the airfield to replace Navy PB-1Ws in service. Negotiations were documented between Texas Railway and the Navy to provide a selection from the B-17s at Altus and consideration of an additional 15 B-17s still at Kingman. Terms worked out provided that Esperado/TREC would get $9,350 for those B-17s at Altus and $9,850 for those at Kingman, which included delivery to, presumably, the Navy facility at Johnsville, Pennsylvania (thus the price difference for the ferry distance). In the end, the Navy decided not to purchase any B-17s from Altus, instead receiving a like number from the AAF.[149]

By early 1948, however, the scrapping operation was moving forward and any warplanes remaining from the original sale were broken apart and smelted on the spot. Evidently the deed was done by May 1948, for at that time the airfield was turned over to the city of Altus for use as a municipal airport.[150] However, the city was not content to lose the economic boost of the military presence, and a lobbying effort was made toward reactivating the airfield. That effort proved successful, and in January 1953, the field was reopened as Altus AFB. Much of the succeeding service has been in missile support of the Strategic Air Command and a major training base for C-5 and C-141 operations. Altus AFB remains active to this day.[151]

The massive single field scrapping operations were complete by the fall of 1948, and with that World War II–era aircraft became rarer and rarer with each passing year. The nation turned its attention to fighting the Korean and Cold Wars, and was captivated by new military aviation technologies, such as the supersonic Century Series fighters and the new, all-jet B-47, B-52, and B-58 bombers. The massive aerial armadas of World War II had passed into history.

CHAPTER 4
Naval Aircraft Storage and Disposal

Naval aircraft disposal policy was extremely different from that of the Army Air Forces. The AAF was positioning its aircraft fleet for the transition to all-jet power, while the U.S. Navy had committed itself to piston-powered aircraft for the foreseeable future. Although the Navy was developing its own jet aircraft, the lack of thrust and reduced range of early jets prevented their immediate adoption for carrier use. In addition, a number of promising piston-powered aircraft were coming into the Navy's inventory at the end of 1945, including the F7F Tigercat and F8F Bearcat. While the AAF was rapidly disposing of its vast B-24 fleet, the U.S. Navy planned to employ the type (PB4Y-1 Liberators and single-tail PB4Y-2 Privateers) into the mid-1950s. The AAF had essentially dropped its requirement for Liberators by late 1943, preferring instead to acquire B-29s and the planned B-36. When Japan surrendered, the Navy still had factory-fresh Privateers moving through the modification lines. These aircraft were subsequently stored at the Naval Air Field in Litchfield Park with only two hours total flying time—a quick test hop and the trip from San Diego to Litchfield Park.

The Navy's reserve of aircraft enabled the service to concentrate its funding demands on developing an ideal carrier-based jet fighter—which eventually developed into the successful F9F Panther/Cougar line—and to acquire new, modern capital ships such as aircraft carriers and advanced submarines. During the late 1940s, the political climate was perceived as a fight to the death between the Navy and Air Force, but the coming Korean conflict gave each service the opportunity to prove its worth.

The Navy, too, had its share of war-weary and obsolete aircraft to delete from its inventory. Most of the major depot-level bases had some form of aircraft storage and scrapping operation, and this included such bases as Alameda, Norfolk, Jacksonville, and San Diego's North Island. By far, the Navy's largest single operation was at NAS Clinton, Oklahoma. It is probably the least known of the large storage depots sold by the WAA in June 1946, yet it was also the largest.

Located approximately 120 miles west of Oklahoma City, NAS Clinton was established as a Naval Air Station in mid-1943. Initial development of the

Bu.No. 149827 was delivered to the Navy in 1961 as one of seven P5M-1T crew trainers. Covered in spraylat, this Martin Marlin awaits scrapping at NAS North Island, San Diego, California, in April 1967. *Armand H. Veronico Collection*

The tactical aircraft inventory at Clinton was 7,547 aircraft, consisting of 264 observation types; 3,852 fighter types; 2,585 light bombers; 666 medium bombers; and 180 heavy bombers. These SB2Cs are only a fraction of the 362 Helldivers that were in storage. *National Archives via Mel Shettle*

An aerial view of Clinton, Oklahoma, in April 1946 when 8,839 aircraft were in storage. Sherman Machine and Iron Works of Oklahoma City won the contract to scrap the field. *National Archives via Mel Shettle*

Another Grumman F11F-1, Bu.No. 141783, on the line. Note the JD-1 Invader parked between it and another Grumman Tiger. *Brian Baker*

With the remnants of its last duty station, Annapolis, painted across the tail, Grumman UF-1T, Bu.No. 131916, is shown in storage in 1961. *Brian Baker*

Douglas F4D-1, Bu.No. 130748, at Litchfield Park. Photographer Brian Baker was one of the few individuals to capture any of the aircraft held in storage on film. In 1961 approximately 1,600 aircraft were held in reserve at the facility. The Navy was evidently much more restrictive on photography than was its counterparts with the USAF at Davis-Monthan AFB. *Brian Baker*

airfield began in October 1942, at a site 19 miles southwest of Clinton. It was developed as a Naval Experimental Station for a drone and remotely controlled aircraft program. The drone program was encompassed by the Training Task Force, a new command established on March 23, 1943, with headquarters at NAS Clinton. The NAS was formally established on June 1, 1943. An aircraft modification program was also established at NAS Clinton. By the spring of 1944, two Navy drone squadrons were in service at NAS Clinton. The drone function ended in November 1944, when the units were dispersed.

Subsequently, the airfield was used as a Navy aircraft storage and salvage facility. By March 1945, the Navy was storing more than 1,000 aircraft on the field.[152] By August 1945, a total of 1,762 aircraft were in storage at NAS Clinton. The Navy

continued to utilize the field in a limited-operational fashion with the transfer of some airfield requirements of the Naval Air Navigation School to NAS Clinton. A large number of the last Navy R4D-7 (DC-3) production of the Douglas-Oklahoma City plant was delivered and subsequently stored at Clinton, with deliveries to operational units from storage stocks as required. However, by December 1945, the Navy had assimilated all the Clinton aircraft it needed, and the station and its remaining stored aircraft were turned over to the RFC for continued use as a storage field.[153]

Although the record is not clear, it is apparent that the entire Naval aircraft inventory present on the airfield on the transfer date was simultaneously declared surplus and released for disposal. By early April 1946, there were 8,839 Naval aircraft on the field being held in storage. The largest number of

Ex-Naval Reserve Memphis PB4Y-2 Privateer Bu.No. 59901 at Litchfield Park in 1960. Both of the aircraft's dorsal turrets, its two waist blister turrets, and the tail turret were removed for Naval Reserve duty. In the early 1960s, many civilian aircraft conversion companies would acquire a surplus PB4Y-2, remove its four R-1830-92 engines, and scrap the fuselage. The engines would then be installed on executive transport DC-3s, making them the Lear Jets of their day. *Milo Peltzer Collection*

these were single-engine F6F Hellcats, FM Wildcats, and Grumman TBM Avengers (see Table 1).[154]

The numbers would suggest that many of the basic trainers, such as the Vultee SNV (BT-13), were sold in April and May 1946. By May 16, 1946, the tactical aircraft inventory at Clinton was 7,547 aircraft, consisting of 264 observation types; 3,852 fighter types; 2,585 light bombers; 666 medium bombers; and 180 heavy bombers.[155] This number was cited by the WAA in the June 18, 1946, announcement for the sale of the contents of the five major tactical storage depots. The terms of the offering specified that the winning contractor would have 12 months to clear Clinton of the aircraft scrap.

On July 1, 1946, the WAA announced that the Sherman Machine and Iron Works Company of Oklahoma City, Oklahoma, was the winning bidder for those tactical aircraft stored at Clinton. The Sherman Machine and Iron Works subsequently became a partner in ACC, and parts that were not available at Walnut Ridge were supplied to the AAF under the same contract through the auspices of TREC.[156]

Table 1

Aircraft Inventory at NAS Clinton, Oklahoma, April 1946

Type	Number	Type	Number
F3A	111	PBJ	331
F4F	2	PBY	1
F4U	435	PV	316
F6F	1,366	RY	9
FG	404	SB2C	362
FM	1,444	SBD	933
JRC	2	SBF	88
N2S	344	SBW	95
OS2N	62	SNV	1,151
OS2U	180	SOC	3
PB4Y	161	TBM/TBF	1,039
		Total	**8,839**

Bu.No. 130411 was 1 of 70 North American Aviation–built AJ-2 Savage twin-engine attack bombers. This aircraft last served with VAH-16, and sits in retirement on April 9, 1958, at Litchfield Park. *Brian Baker*

Sherman Machine and Iron Works, besides selling equipment back to the government, also sold a number of aircraft on the civil market for flyable purposes in exception to the "scrap only" provisions of the original WAA sale contract. At least three Navy PBJs were sold to U.S. civil owners by Sherman in November 1946.[157] However, available records suggest that only a few aircraft survived the scrapping operation conducted at Clinton in 1947.

On January 27, 1949, the Naval Air Station was deeded to the city of Clinton by the WAA. Its status for the subsequent five years is unknown, but it was probably used as a municipal airport. On September

Scrapping operations at NAS Norfolk used a 6,100-pound chopping blade to reduce aircraft into manageable pieces. A Navy press release stated that four operators could reduce 16 aircraft per day into scrap. In 1947 this OS2U-3 Kingfisher's carcass was part of 397 railroad cars of scrap metal produced during the year. *U.S. Navy*

The Defense Department wanted to save money and was under the impression that a single aircraft could meet the needs of both the Navy and Air Force. The result was the F-111—highly successful in Air Force service, but not built to withstand the rigor of carrier duty. After thorough testing, this F-111B-CF, one of nine prototypes, is ready for reclamation. The Navy F-111s differed from Air Force examples, having shorter nose cones, wider wings, and provisions for six AIM-54A Phoenix missiles. *Brian Baker*

15, 1954, however, the field was reclaimed by the federal government as allowed by the terms of the original deed and turned over for use by the U.S. Air Force. In 1955 additional acreage was procured and the site was established as the Clinton-Sherman AFB. The main north-south runway was rebuilt as a 13,500-foot concrete heavy bomber runway for use by B-58s of the Strategic Air Command (SAC). The base was finally closed in 1970, and the field reverted to civil use in August 1972. As of 1999, there was talk of turning the expansive air base into a space shuttle port.

NAF Litchfield Park

The Defense Plant Corporation built a large facility for use by the Goodyear Aircraft Corporation as a modification center at Litchfield Park, Arizona, in 1943. Located approximately 20 miles west of Phoenix, the Navy constructed a single 6,000-foot landing strip next to the Goodyear facility and established an Auxiliary Aircraft Acceptance Unit on the field. The Goodyear plant was used to modify Army B-24s, built at the Consolidated plant at San Diego, California, for use as Navy PB4Y-1s. The facility was also used to accept 556 single-tail PB4Y-2 Privateers for the Navy.[158] In December 1944, the airfield was designated as NAF Litchfield Park.[159]

At the conclusion of the war, the Goodyear plant was closed and station operations were reduced significantly. Approximately 250 aircraft, primarily PB4Y-2s that were being processed for delivery as the war ended, were stored on the field pending a determination of postwar plans. In addition, aircraft processed through overhaul shops were sent to Litchfield Park for short-term storage while awaiting reassignment.

Four YTP-34-P-12A turboprop-powered Lockheed Constellations were built, two for the Navy as R7V-2s (Bu.Nos. 131630 and 131631) and a pair for the Air Force designated C-121Fs. R7V-2 131630 has been preserved for long-term storage in this March 14, 1958, photo. *Brian Baker*

Litchfield Park saw a tremendous influx of aircraft at war's end. In the foreground, more than 100 F4U Corsairs of various models await a new mission, while across the runway to the right, factory-fresh PB4Y-2s and P2V Neptunes sit awaiting the next call to duty. *San Diego Aerospace Museum*

At NAS Jacksonville this PBY Catalina, an early flying boat, teeters back onto its tail with its nose held high in the air by its beaching gear. Although many PBY-5 and later-model amphibian Catalinas were sold to the surplus civil market, none of the true flying boats survived. *National Archives*

With the Kennedy Administration and Secretary of Defense Robert McNamara came efforts at standardizing the military services. This is reflected by the common aircraft designation system implemented in 1962, and attempts at common aircraft types for both the Navy and Air Force—such as the General Dynamics F-111. The Department of Defense also decided to consolidate military aircraft storage facilities and created, in 1965, the Military Aircraft Storage and Disposition Center (MASDC) at Davis-Monthan AFB near Tucson, Arizona. Of the aircraft in storage at Litchfield Park, approximately 800 were moved, either by air or by truck, to Davis-Monthan between February 1965 and June 1966.[165] The remaining inventory, numbering approximately 1,000 aircraft, was declared excess to any possible future military requirements. They were then salvaged for parts and the remains sold to the highest bidder.

NAF Litchfield Park was disestablished as a Navy facility in January 1967. The airport, operated by the city of Phoenix, has since become a major training facility and reliever airfield for Phoenix Sky Harbor. The old Goodyear plant remains intact but any evidence of the Navy aircraft stored on the field between 1945 and 1966 is long gone.

CHAPTER 5
Davis-Monthan: From Aircraft Storage to Aircraft Recycling

When planning for demobilization at the end of World War II, the AAF determined that a parallel system for managing surplus aircraft should be developed. One system would dispose of war-weary and obsolete aircraft through the RFC and the WAA, while the other would store aircraft for future use by the Army Air Corps.

AAF Regulation 65-86, dated June 14, 1944, charged the Air Service Command and the Material Command (merged on August 31, 1944, to form the ATSC—Air Technical Service Command) with selecting locations for the storage and disposal of surplus aircraft. ATSC also maintained each plane from the time it left squadron service until its final disposition, whether it was placed into reserve or sold as surplus.

One level higher in the chain of command was Wright Field, Ohio's Aircraft Distribution Office (ADO). The ADO determined which aircraft types the ATSC was to store or dispose of, how many, and their serial numbers. The ADO also, under direction from the Assistant Chief of Air Staff, Operations, Commitments, and Requirements, removed from storage those aircraft needed to meet current requirements, including foreign military assistance.

Establishing an Aircraft Reserve

During the spring of 1945, the ATSC was storing aircraft at any depot with excess acreage. It was quickly learned that fields located near the coasts, such as Mobile, Alabama; Oakland, California; and Miami, Florida, were unsuitable due to the rapid onset of corrosion and rust. Depots in the snowbelt—Rome and Syracuse, New York; and Middletown, Pennsylvania—were subject to costly delays when

in- or out-processing aircraft due to weather conditions. Eight depots—Mobile, Alabama; Middletown, Pennsylvania; Sacramento and San Bernadino, California; Warner Robins, Georgia; Oklahoma City, Oklahoma; San Antonio, Texas; and Ogden, Utah—were forced to receive aircraft for storage, although this was an imposition on the bases' primary duty of aircraft overhaul and maintenance.

The remedy to weather and workload problems was the establishment of "specialized storage fields" within the continental United States "for the primary purpose of storing reserves of aircraft (and for the processing and disposition of excess and surplus aircraft) and not open for transient traffic or repairs or

Sweet Thing, a beautiful representation of World War II nose art, adorns this unidentified B-29 in storage at Davis-Monthan in 1946. *R. F. Schirmer/American Aviation Historical Society*

Sixty-five engineless B-36 Peacemakers dominate more than 200 C-47s and more than 100 precariously perched Republic F-84 Thunderjets in this late 1959 aerial photo. *AMARC photo*

Bernadino, Hobbs, South Plains, Independence, and Garden City were closed that year, with Victorville following in 1948. San Bernadino was reopened in 1949, and Middletown was closed in 1950.[169]

The first year of the new decade saw the ATSC's storage activities concentrated at two specialized storage facilities, Davis-Monthan and Pyote, and six storage depots: Ogden (Hill Air Force Base); Oklahoma City (Tinker AFB); San Antonio (Kelly AFB); San Bernadino (Norton AFB); Sacramento (McClellan AFB); and Warner Robins Air Materiel Areas.

Determining How to Store an Aircraft: The Cocoon

Prior to World War II, the AAF of planes. But after the Japanese surrender, it was a different story. While fighting the battle to locate sufficient parking space for the service's reserve aircraft, a method to preserve the planes had to be developed. The AAF and ATSC began to develop maintenance and preservation procedures as well as storage classifications.

The first procedure was to determine an aircraft's status: Class I, strategic reserve; Class II, operational reserve; Class III, excess; and Class IV, surplus. Once an aircraft's status was ascertained, it was placed into one of four types of storage: Type A, short term–ready to fly within 72 hours; Type B, indefinite temporary storage–available for operations within seven days; Type C, extended storage; and Type D, storage of temporarily ground aircraft. As a matter of practice, Class I aircraft were placed into Type A storage; Class II into Type B; and Class III and IV into Type C storage. If an aircraft was taken off operational status without a class determination being made, it was placed into Type D storage.[170]

In an effort to maintain the condition of aircraft in storage, a "cocooning" program was developed. Cocooning was envisioned as a way to reduce airframe

The first two coats of the insulmastic cocoon, yellow, then red, cover the tail of a B-29 at Davis-Monthan. A black Gilsonite coating was followed by a white coat to reflect the sun's rays, thereby reducing the humidity inside the aircraft. *R. F. Schirmer/American Aviation Historical Society*

corrosion, interior and systems deterioration, and at the same time lower maintenance costs. The cocooning effort was started on April 11, 1946, under the direction of ATSC's Maintenance Division, which had sent a directive to the Engineering Division, Headquarters AMC, to develop a means to maintain a constant humidity in B-29 cockpits.[171] The B-29, America's atom bomber, was a high-priority aircraft during the transition from piston- to jet-powered aircraft, and maintaining adequate stocks of the bomber was vital to national defense.

The Engineering Division developed three potential preservation programs: storing aircraft in air-conditioned buildings; storing in hermetically sealed containers; and applying removable plastic coatings.[172] The Navy had attempted to preserve large numbers of fighters in many of its former airship hangars, and found that they could not reduce humidity below 50 percent. The Navy had also tested containerizing a number of fighter aircraft, but this suggestion would not work for the AAF, which had

In the cocooning process, all of the openings were taped to seal any window or turret fuselage joints. Taping is used to build up the area from the cowling nose bowl to the propeller spinner. The amount of scaffolding and 55-gallon drums makes the process look unorganized by today's standards. *R. F. Schirmer/American Aviation Historical Society*

The first coat was almost transparent, as evidenced by the star and bar showing through the yellow insulmastic. The worker on the top scaffolding is nearly 20 feet in the air. In December 1948, Davis-Monthan had more than 450 cocooned B-29s in storage. Most of these aircraft would be recalled for the Korean War two years later. *R. F. Schirmer/American Aviation Historical Society*

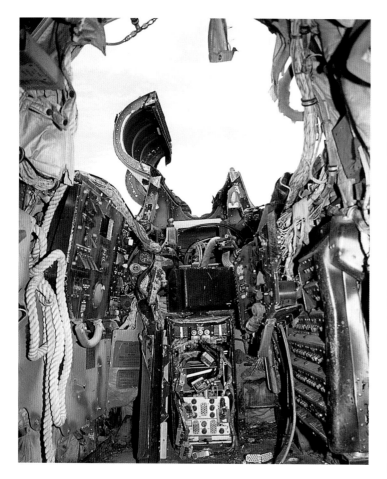

After all usable parts were stripped from the B-52s, including the cockpit and tail gunner's compartment, they were cut into five sections to comply with START. *Nicholas A. Veronico*

more than 1,000 B-29s to preserve. The other problem was to find enough suitable containers to store an aircraft with a fuselage length of 99 feet and a wing span of 141.2 feet.

The third suggested method of aircraft preservation proposed by the Engineering Division was endorsed by the Naval Ordnance Division and the Battelle Institute. In July 1946, a number of B-29s were cocooned at Warner Robins to determine the costs of manpower and preservative materials. AMC knew that it would cost $11,228,760 to maintain 2,221 aircraft in unprotected storage for 15 months. Based on these figures, AMC believed nearly $6 million could be saved using the cocooning method. On August 15, $2 million worth of cocooning materials were purchased, and an additional $3 million was authorized to maintain the aircraft for 15 months.[173] The Fort Pitt Packaging Company and the J. I. Hass Company were awarded contracts to supply labor for the cocooning efforts, while the materials were supplied by AMC.[174]

To cocoon a B-29 bomber, contractors installed 1,300 pounds of silica gel desiccant and humidity indicators in the aircraft, covered all openings with tape, which was followed by red and yellow layers of sprayed-on plastic. A black Gilsonite (asphalt-based) covering, known as insulmastic, was applied over the plastic, which was finally sealed with an aluminum-colored paint. Clear plastic windows were left in the cocoon to allow the aircraft's interior to be monitored.

At the end of April 1948, there were 166 cocooned B-29s at Warner Robins, 378 at Davis-Monthan, 73 at Pyote, and 38 at Sacramento. An additional 94 B-29s were moving through the cocooning process when, on May 13, 1948, Headquarters (AMC) discontinued cocooning operations. Those aircraft that were more than halfway cocooned were completed, while the balance were stripped and returned to storage.[175] The decision to discontinue cocooning was due to excessive ballooning and blistering of the cocooning plastic. In theory, during the heat of the day, the red and yellow plastic layers could be stretched more than three times their length, and then elastically return to their original size. Unfortunately, the black insulmastic's elastic properties would not allow the plastic to return to the original

The saga of B-52D, 55-0678: the Stratofortress arrived at AMARC from the 2nd Bomb Wing on October 17, 1978. Fifteen years later, on July 20, 1993, the bomber sat in a sea of tall tails awaiting elimination under START. The bomber was eliminated under the terms of the treaty on March 1, 1994, and was spotted in a nearby scrapyard on May 11, 1996. *Nicholas A. Veronico*

size when the weather cooled, leaving stretched and sagging material. With repeated heating and cooling, oftentimes the cocoons would stretch more than 100 square feet and had to be replaced.

Nine months after the cocooning project began, an aircraft was opened for inspection and found to be in an excellent state of preservation. Engine cylinders were examined for rust, and none was found. During the time in storage, the interior humidity of the B-29 had varied greatly and it was determined that the desiccant packages did not need to be changed unless conditions were "severe."[176] The biggest problem with cocooning was the removal of its multiple layers. Outside air temperatures at Warner Robins averaged 40 degrees, and although engine heaters were blowing on the cocooning material, the brittle plastic broke into small pieces. Stripping each aircraft took an uneconomical 600 man-hours.

Storage costs calculated in December 1949 showed that the per-day maintenance cost per cocooned B-29 ran $3.71. In contrast, it cost $6.67 per day for a noncocooned Superfortress. These numbers reflect operations at Davis-Monthan and are deceiving due to the dry climate in the Arizona desert. Aircraft cocooned at Pyote and Warner Robins had to be recocooned and, as time wore on, increasing amounts of moisture were transferred through the cocoons as the plastic deteriorated. Cocooned B-29s were maintained until the end of 1957, when the B-29 fleet was consigned to the smelter.

Pyote: Bad Weather, Fleeting Workforce

During World War II, Pyote Army Air Field was a B-17 replacement crew training base that later transitioned to the B-29 near war's end. The base's storage inventory began with B-29s, P-63s, L-4, and L-5

Stacked two and three high, B-52 fuselages wait their turn in the aluminum shredder at a nearby scrap dealer. The aluminum is then shipped out of state to be recycled. *Nicholas A. Veronico*

This 13,000-pound guillotine blade is dropped from 80 feet onto the Superfortresses to eliminate them from the roles of flyable aircraft. In all, 365 B-52s will be scrapped to comply with START. *Nicholas A. Veronico*

liaison aircraft. Eventually, B-17s, F-13 photo reconnaissance versions of the B-29, A-26s, and B-25s were also stored at the West Texas base.

At the end of the war, the base had a staff of 441. Nearby oil fields were paying high salaries and lured away many of the men. This drain of experienced workers, and the inability to hire new ones, resulted in poor quality of workmanship in the cocooning operation. Officers at the San Antonio Air Material

Area wrote scathing reports of the project and the condition of the planes, including reports of cocooned aircraft with wing tips exposed.[177] Cocooning had expanded so much that it drooped and moved with the wind.

Labor difficulties and poor workmanship were aggravated by Pyote's weather conditions. Two studies on humidity at Pyote were conducted—each resulting in a diametrically opposed answer. One claimed that "the absence of humidity results in no corrosion on the aircraft," while the other stated that the "relative humidity is high enough to cause some corrosion."[178] A third study cited the United States Weather Station at Vandalia, Ohio, as recording the average relative humidity as 75 percent at 7 A.M., the perfect conditions for corrosion. The storms of West Texas did not win any votes for Pyote becoming the Air Force's single continental U.S. storage site either. On August 9, 1948, a tornado and an associated hailstorm damaged 90 percent of the

Blue Angels A-4 Skyhawk Bu.No 154179 sits on pallets ready for delivery to a waiting museum. This fighter arrived at AMARC on February 13, 1985, shortly after the Blue Angels transitioned into the F/A-18 Hornet. A-4s flew with the Blue Angels from 1974 to 1985 and the nimble fighter thrilled millions of spectators. Aircraft of the demonstration squadron were stripped of all combat gear and, after lightening the Skyhawk, the team had a 11,300-pound airplane with an engine that produced 11,400 pounds thrust. This thrust-to-weight ratio explains how the team performed so many outstanding maneuvers in the A-4. *Nicholas A. Veronico*

aircraft in storage—resulting in the total write-off of eight aircraft.[179]

As a storage center, Pyote was headed for closure. The AMC began to examine Pyote's cost structure and was faced with answering the question of whether the inefficient field, unable to attract a quality workforce, should be closed. Another option was to turn the operation over to a commercial enterprise. In January 1950, Grand Central Aircraft Co. of Tucson submitted the lowest proposal to operate the storage facility at Pyote, under contract to AMC. After review, it was believed that Grand Central's workforce estimates were too low, and the bid was rejected. On March 24, 1950, the Pyote Management Board was formed. Headed by John Myer, the board traveled to the field to review operations. They

This two-seat F-100F 56-4001 was removed from storage and is being prepared for flight to Mojave in January 1990, where it was converted into a target drone. This Super Sabre entered storage on September 28, 1979, and was last flown by the 118th Tactical Fighter Squadron, Connecticut Air National Guard. *Karen B. Haack*

Convair F-102A-80 Delta Dagger, serial number 56-1455, has been sitting in the Arizona sun since its arrival on May 13, 1971. Eight-hundred seventy-five F-102As were built at Convair's San Diego factory during the mid-1950s, and 56-1455 last flew with the 57th Fighter Interceptor Squadron. When this May 1996 photo was taken, only three F-102s were in storage; the remainder were converted to drones, moved to bombing ranges to serve as targets, or scrapped. *Nicholas A. Veronico*

immediately cut 230 workers from the payroll, and began to examine how the leaner workforce could achieve its operational goals.[180]

Political events outside the United States determined Pyote's short-term fate. North Korea's June 25, 1950, invasion of South Korea focused the Air Force's attention away from the troubles and onto the aircraft parked at the West Texas storage site.

Davis-Monthan: The Ideal Storage Site

On November 15, 1945, Davis-Monthan AAF was transferred from the 2nd Air Force to the command of the San Antonio ATSC (SAATSC), and the field was slated to become a B-29 storage facility. The 4105th AAF Base Unit (Aircraft Storage) managed the influx of aircraft slated for long-term preservation. Unlike Pyote, the wind rarely, if ever, blew more than 50 miles per hour, and the relative humidity only got as high as 51 percent. The workforce stood at 1,245,

In 1969 the USMC bought 102 Vertical Take Off and Landing AV-8As and eight TAV-8A two-seat trainers. The Harrier, as it was christened, was selected for its ability to operate from front-line, unimproved air strips as well as assault landing ships, which have limited deck space. Deliveries of the AV-8A began in January 1971 to VMA-513. Photographed in May 1996, Bu.No. 158977 last served with VMA-542—the second squadron to receive Harriers—and was stored at AMARC on April 3, 1986, and was still in storage in March 2000. This aircraft was bought as an AV-8A and modernized in lieu of the Marine Corps purchasing new aircraft. The program called for the AV-8As to receive tail warning radar, chaff/flare dispensers to defeat surface-to-air missiles, and improved aerodynamic lift devices, which included a modified horizontal forward flap and strakes under the fuselage. These modifications brought the aircraft up to AV-8C standards. *Nicholas A. Veronico*

and the labor market was deemed "reasonably good."[181] On January 10, 1946, the 4105th took delivery of its first C-47 for extended storage.[182]

On March 15, the Continental Air Command ceased to exist and the SAC, of which the 2nd Air Force was a component, and the Tactical Air Command were formed. On April 1, command of Davis-Monthan Field was returned to the 2nd Air Force, whereby SAATSC became a tenant organization.[183] SAC wanted exclusive use of the field to train B-29 crews and, unfortunately, the weather that is ideal for aircraft storage is also the best for flight training. SAC instructed ATSC to remove its aircraft from the base as soon as possible, and headquarters AMC began working toward that goal. The number of planes arriving for storage was drastically reduced and Air Force requests for reserve aircraft were filled from 4105th stocks first if possible.

At the end of 1946, the 4105th was maintaining the following aircraft in storage: 679 B-29s, 241 C-47s, and 30 aircraft slated for the future Air Force

Republic RF-84F, 53-7600, is a photo reconnaissance version of the Thunderstreak known as the Thunderflash, and last served with the 106th Tactical Reconnaissance Squadron of the Alabama Air National Guard. Only two F-84s were in storage when this photo was taken in May 1996. *Nicholas A. Veronico*

This F-100F (421), serial number 56-3837, was last flown by the Indiana Air National Guard's 163rd Tactical Fighter Squadron. The Super Sabre was retired on September 26, 1979, when the type was phased out of National Guard service. On August 28, 1990, 56-3837 was flown to Mojave to be converted into a QF-100F drone, but was returned to AMARC before the work was completed. The majority of those aircraft returned from the drone program have been placed on display. Of the aircraft in this May 1996 photo, "416" has been moved to Lineville, Alabama, for display, while "417," "420," and "421" were at AMARC in March 2000. *Nicholas A. Veronico*

Executive-configured Douglas VC-54E, serial number 44-9117, wears the markings of its last operator, the 198th Tactical Fighter Squadron, Puerto Rico Air National Guard. When this September 11, 1976, photo was taken, World War II–vintage C-54s were often sold in flyable condition as the military had no need for their parts. Desert Air Parts of Tucson acquired the aircraft on August 20, 1979, and most likely sold it off piece by piece to cargo haulers and fire bombers still operating the type. *Brian Baker*

Five months after its retirement on November 6, 1975, RF-101C, serial number 56-0060, from the 165th Tactical Reconnaissance Squadron, Kentucky Air National Guard sits in storage along the fence near Escalante Road on the base's north side. In May 1995, this aircraft was shipped to Holloman Air Force Base, New Mexico, for display. *Brian Baker*

museum.[184] The museum collection included the sole Douglas B-19, Wendell Wilkie's C-87, a Consolidated Vultee B-32 Dominator, the Beech XC-38 Destroyer equipped with a 75-mm cannon, and an XCG-17 glider version of the Douglas C-47. Only the B-24D *Strawberry Bitch*, the B-29s *Enola Gay* and *Bock's Car*, a German Ju-88, and President Franklin D. Roosevelt's C-54 *Sacred Cow* were saved.[185]

During the first four months of 1947, the 4105th was busy reorganizing its stored aircraft by type, in groups of 10 aircraft, to improve fire safety and maintenance efficiency. By the end of April, all aircraft had been repositioned. On July 18, the AMC was instructed to vacate Davis-Monthan as soon as possible. By November, SAC had agreed to let cocooned war reserve aircraft remain at the field "until it was necessary to return them to service."[186]

As Cold War tensions increased in the early months of 1948, 100 B-29s—some from storage—

Fifteen of the 17 GTD-21s were lined up on July 20, 1993, after 2 had been shipped to the U.S. Air Force Museum for display. Four of the drones have gone to NASA Dryden for a possible research program while others have gone to museums, including Pima Air and Space Museum, Tucson, Arizona; Museum of Flight, Seattle, Washington; as well as Beale and Warner Robins Air Force Bases. *Nicholas A. Veronico*

were sent to modification centers under the Gem program. These aircraft were modified under the "Saddletree" program, enabling them to carry atomic weapons. New avionics, electronics, radar, and communication equipment was also installed. Other 38 B-29s were removed from Oklahoma City, Warner Robins, Pyote, and Davis-Monthan for "Superman" and "Ruralist" air-to-air refueling modifications.

An additional 302 B-29s were called up from storage for SAC use under three projects with a combined budget of $13.8 million. On October 18, a request for all Wright R-3350-57s fitted with master controls and fuel injection were to be removed from aircraft at Pyote and Davis-Monthan to support B-29 operations with SAC.[187]

Although AMC had tried to reduce the 4105th's inventory, 683 aircraft were on the field at the beginning of 1949. Gen. G. W. Mundy, Headquarters AMC–Supply and Maintenance Division, attempted to negotiate with SAC. The general pleaded his case: AMC had only two dedicated storage sites (Pyote and

A newly arrived GTD-21 supersonic drone designed to be air-launched from the back of a Lockheed A-12 (predecessor to the SR-71). This photograph was taken on October 8, 1977, within a year of the drone's arrival. Interestingly enough, once spraylat had been applied, the GTD-21s were declared secret—after many visitors had seen them on the base's public tours. *Brian Baker*

This pair of Douglas C-47s is being processed out of storage for the Vietnam War, March 2, 1967. *AMARC photo*

In December 1969, this Superfortress, the last at Davis-Monthan, was parked on "Celebrity Row" where the more unusual aircraft are displayed near the fence line. B-29A, 44-70016, was later transferred from the base to form the nucleus of the Pima Air Museum, which opened to the public on May 8, 1976. *Pima Air and Space Museum*

Davis-Monthan); all storage depots were full; and that Davis-Monthan was the ideal storage site. In spite of General Mundy's attempts to remain on the field, he was given a copy of the July 18, 1947, eviction notice and instructed to act upon it. SAC wanted to build dependent housing on the site, and suggested that AMC purchase 640 acres east of the base for aircraft storage. On August 28, 1948, the 4105th was redesignated the 3040th Aircraft Storage Depot and aircraft reclamation and salvage were added to the unit's mission. On October 5, the 3040th's name was changed from Aircraft Storage Depot to Aircraft Storage Squadon. Like all other military organizations of the time, everything was put on hold to support the Korean conflict.

Korean War Operations

Immediate war needs required transport aircraft, and Davis-Monthan had plenty of C-47s in storage for just such an emergency. In the first three weeks of the conflict, 47 C-47s were flown to the San Bernardino Air Depot for overhaul and shipment overseas. An additional 37 C-47s were dispatched from Davis-Monthan in September and October. Also, 27 Davis-Monthan B-29s were to be salvaged, and their parts returned to inventory. When the Superfortresses were stored in 1947, their value was listed as $570,000 each. Reclamation returned between $270,000 and $350,000 worth of parts per plane. The need for B-29s and their associated parts saw Davis-Monthan's inventory drop to only 237 B-29s of which 65 were not cocooned. Within the storage system, 200 B-29s were reclaimed for spares to support the Stratofortress fleet.[188]

On July 30, the Air Force transferred 150 F-51Ds from Air Guard units to the Far East Air Force in support of Korean operations. On August 7, 180 F-51Ds were ordered removed from storage, and this number was subsequently revised upward to 267. These aircraft replaced those lost by the Air National Guard and a number were transferred to Canada. The remaining 205 F-51Hs were removed from storage to supplement the Air Guard, thereby eliminating the type from aircraft reserves. By the end of 1950, more than 500 F-51s had been removed from storage to support the Korean War effort.

During the same time frame, 396 Douglas B-26s were removed from storage—the majority from stocks at Pyote—and also sent to Korea. To support these aircraft with spare parts, 167 B-26s were salvaged. The Sacramento Air Materiel Area also provided 28 F-80s and 23 RF-80s from storage stocks to support the Far East Air Force's efforts in Korea.

The end of the Korean War saw a reversal in operations. Davis-Monthan had only 207 B-29s and three museum aircraft on its inventory in June 1953. At the end of the year, an additional 771 aircraft had arrived for storage including 120 AT-6s, 29 SA-16 Albatross air-sea rescue amphibians, 13 L-20

In 1959 the Air Force was scrapping planes as quickly as it could to make room for a coming influx of aircraft. The massive B-36 fleet was on its way to the smelter, and these early Republic F-84s were, by this time, obsolete. Supersonic F-100s, F-101s, and F-102s—to mention but three types—had taken over front-line duties in the Air Force replacing the subsonic, straight-wing F-84Bs. *Both photos Pima Air and Space Museum*

An aerial view of the AMARC industrial complex with A-7s and F-4s in the foreground and Titan II missile storage to the left. The reclamation shelter is 918 feet long and has 180,072 square feet under cover, enabling aircraft to be processed on the hottest of days. *Nicholas A. Veronico*

This B-58A, serial number 58-2433, is missing its nose radome, two canopy covers, engines, and various inspection panels in this October 9, 1976, photo. The entire B-58 fleet was scrapped beginning in May 1977 when the bombers were sold as a lot to Southwestern Alloys. *Brian Baker*

Beavers, and 21 radio-controlled QB-17 drones. To provide parking space for this influx of aircraft, 480 acres of land were acquired at a cost of $24,000—bringing the 3040th's acreage to 1,290.[189]

The aircraft reserve fleet proved its worth during the Korean War. The Air Force had a ready source of aircraft and spare parts, thus providing front-line commanders with an effective fighting tool. During the Korean War, B-29s flew 21,328 sorties, dropping 167,000 tons of bombs, 1,995 reconnaissance and 797 psychological warfare missions.[190]

Air Force Storage Consolidation

In the summer of 1952, the AMC's Maintenance and Engineering Division was studying operations at Pyote. The Engineering Division determined that the facility should remain open since it would not be effective to close the base and move its fleet of 317 B-29s—at a cost of $10 million. The point became moot when the B-29 was declared obsolete.

Simultaneously, on May 21, 1954, the 3040th Aircraft Storage Squadron, Davis-Monthan AFB, was designated as the Air Force's sole aircraft storage facility in the continental United States.[191] The last SAC B-29, an "A" model assigned to the 307th Bomb Wing, Kadena Air Base, Okinawa, arrived at Davis-Monthan on November 4, 1954.[192] Having no further need for the B-29, Pyote's inventory was eliminated at the hands of a smelter, and Davis-Monthan truly became the Air Force's only aircraft storage facility.

While the B-29s were awaiting the scrapper's torch, SAC began converting to B-52s in June 1956. With the announcement of the B-36's phaseout, the first 53 of the giant bombers began arriving at Davis-Monthan by the end of August. On June 1, 1956, the 3040th was redesignated as the Arizona Aircraft Storage Branch (AASB) and transferred to the San Bernardino Air Materiel Area. In September, SAC agreed to operate Davis-Monthan AFB on a joint tenancy agreement with AMC, provided AASB's primary mission remain Class III and IV storage. The battle for a permanent home was over.

To make room for the huge B-36 bombers, the B-29s would have to be salvaged. Page Airways and

Aircraft Associates were running two furnaces to process B-29s. On February 21, 1958, AASB authorized two additional sweaters, which were constructed by National Metal Co., and in July AASB paid $30,000 for Aircraft Associates' furnace. With three sweaters under AASB control, one was now assigned to each salvage contract. The contractor was responsible for renovating and maintaining the government-owned sweater over the life of the scrapping contract. Six B-29s could be processed in a day, turning out 65,000 pounds of aluminum.[193] The last B-36 was flown from Davis-Monthan to the Air Force Museum, Wright-Patterson AFB, Ohio, on April 29, 1959—less than two years later, on July 25, 1961, the last B-36 was chopped into pieces. The entire fleet of B-36s had been processed into ingots.[194]

On July 1, 1959, the inventory of aircraft stored at Davis-Monthan numbered 4,154. This wealth of aircraft represented the tools to fight the spread of communism. Through the Military Assistance Program and foreign military sales, friendly governments were able to acquire aircraft from America's surplus stocks. On August 21, the Mexican government bought 30 T-28s, and additional T-28s, C-47s, and B-26s were pulled from storage for use in Southeast Asia. In addition, Guatemala, Belgium, Denmark,

On Mark Engineering Co. of Van Nuys, California, modified a World War II–era A-26 Invader for counterinsurgency operations, and subsequently received an order for 40 aircraft designated B-26Ks. Called the "Counter Invader," the aircraft featured a strengthened wing, eight underwing hard points, eight nose-mounted .50-caliber machine guns, and new R-2800-103W engines. All of the B-26Ks had been processed out of storage by April 1977. *Brian Baker*

Douglas A-1E Skyraider, Bu.No 133860, in Vietnam camouflage on March 27, 1971. This Skyraider's last operator was the 1st Special Operations Wing. Ex-Navy Skyraiders were employed in the ground attack role by the Air Force during the Vietnam War. *Brian Baker*

This two-seat Lockheed F-104D, serial number 57-1333, was equipped with a General Electric J79-GE-7 engine and, although flown in a trainer configuration, could be armed with a pair of AIM-9B Sidewinder missiles. The only item the "D" model lacked was the six-barrel 20-mm cannon. This aircraft arrived for storage on December 11, 1973, was photographed on February 14, 1975, and was sold surplus on March 11, 1982. *Brian Baker*

France, Chile, Brazil, Peru, Argentina, Bolivia, Iceland, Colombia, and Italy purchased aircraft ranging from F-80s, F-84s, and F-86s to T-6s, T-28s, and T-33s, to C-45s, C-46s, C-47s, and C-119s. The Agency for International Development also provided cargo-carrying aircraft for humanitarian operations for friendly foreign governments including Ethiopia, Israel, Peru, Somalia, Spain, Cameroon, and Morocco.[195]

On August 1, 1959, the AASB became the 2704th Air Force Aircraft Storage and Disposition Group (later AF Storage and Disposition Group) under AMC, which was headquartered at Wright-Patterson AFB, Ohio. Eight months later, on April 1, 1961, AMC was separated into two commands: Air Force Logistics Command (AFLC) and Air Force Systems Command; the 2704th became a subordinate command of AFLC.

By the end of 1962, 3,537 aircraft carcasses has been smelted in the government's three sweaters, with $6,159,377.19 returned to the treasury. During fiscal year 1962, for every dollar spent on aircraft reclamation, salvage, and parts redistribution by the 2704th, $70 was saved. To facilitate parts recycling, a new $590,000 reclamation shelter was completed in 1962. This 918-foot-long shelter placed 180,072 square feet of work space in the shade, enabling an aircraft to be parked under it, have all necessary parts removed, cleaned, packaged, and shipped out, and the plane returned to storage. The area around the shelter, 650,000 square feet, was graded, packed, and seal-coated to accommodate aircraft awaiting their turn at reclamation.[196]

By mid-1960, B-47s were slowly arriving at Davis-Monthan for storage and reclamation. SAC's Project Fast Fly accelerated the B-47's retirement along with its KC-97 refueling tanker. Fast Fly's retirement schedule called for 294 B-47s, 118 KC-97s, and 33 B-52s to be retired at a rate of 4 B-47s, 2 KC-97s, and 1 B-52 per day. Although KC-97s would fly with Air Guard units for a number of years to come, subsonic aircraft had fallen out of favor with the Air Force. SAC's last B-47E arrived at Davis-Monthan on February 11, 1966, and they were followed on December 29, 1967, by the last RB-47H, serial number 53-4296—exactly 20 years after the type's first flight.[197]

Times of Change: Single Manager Operating Agency

In a cost-cutting effort, the Department of Defense determined that all aircraft should be stored and maintained at a central location. From this directive, the Assistant Secretary of Defense for Installations and Logistics informed the Assistant Secretary of the Navy on December 28, 1963, that the Air Force had been assigned the responsibility for storage, disposal, and reclamation of all military aircraft, and that this would be accomplished at Davis-Monthan. The memo also called for Litchfield Park's closing. On September 10, 1964, the plan to merge storage activities under the 2704th was approved, and the process of moving planes from Litchfield Park to Davis-Monthan, 150 miles away, began.

An unidentified B-47 Stratojet heads for the chopping blades and then into the furnace at Davis-Monthan. The practice of smelting aircraft on the field ended in the mid-1970s. *R. F. Schirmer/ American Aviation Historical Society*

Aircraft in Storage June 30, 1966	
Model	**Total**
A-1E	87
A-3	35
A-4	40
B-26	7
B-47	1,003
KB-50	63
B-52	31
B-57	1
B-66	41
C-45	153
C-46	3
C-47	106
C-54	117
C-97	215
C-117	5
C-119	198
C-121	42
F-1	10
F-3	46
F-8	58
F-9	10
F-10	1
F-11	7
F-80	—
F-84	4
F-86	177
F-89	116
F-100	34
H-13	2
H-16	19
H-21	79
H-43	39
O-1C	1
P-2	102
S-2	85
T-1	18
T-33	537
T-34	26
U-6	—
RIT*	225
Museum	8
Total	2,929

Note: * RIT (Reclamation Insurance Type) is a special category of aircraft that have been stripped to the major fuselage components. These aircraft provide large structural assemblies such as wings, fuselage sections, or horizontal and vertical surfaces.

While the aircraft were readied for flight or trucked to Tucson, on February 1, 1965, the 2704th ceased to exist and was replaced by the Military Aircraft Storage and Disposition Center. MASDC was to provide a "single operation for processing and maintaining aircraft in storage; preparation of aircraft for one-time flight, transfer, or inspection; reclamation of aircraft/aircraft engines and components for inventory replenishment and/or special projects; processing of aircraft/aircraft engines and residue for disposal; administration of sales and/or service contracts with foreign governments, other governmental agencies, and commercial contractors; and perform field level maintenance on selected aircraft systems and components."[198]

As MASDC's mission was changing, the Navy was busy clearing out Litchfield Park. A total of 4 727 aircraft were transferred to Davis-Monthan—615 by air and 112 by truck. During its history as a storage facility from 1946 to 1966, Litchfield Park processed more than 17,000 aircraft.[199] On September 19, 1966, at 10 A.M., the last plane flew out of NAF Litchfield.[200]

The Navy established a field service office at MASDC, and the Army signed on to have its aircraft maintained at Davis-Monthan on March 29, 1966.

When Litchfield Park was closed as a storage base on September 10, 1964, plans got under way to move the Navy's aircraft 150 miles south to Davis-Monthan. The majority flew to MASDC, but many—including this trio of T-34Bs—were trucked to Tucson. The aircraft in this photo include Bu. Nos. 144035, 144088, and 144030. *Brian Baker*

After serving with the 55th Strategic Reconnaissance Wing, RB-47H, 53-4304, was transferred to Davis-Monthan for storage on November 17, 1965, as the entire fleet was being phased out of the Air Force's inventory. This aircraft was subsequently transferred to the Navy on April 7, 1977, as a source of parts for the Navy's two flying B-47Es (52-4100 and 52-4120). On April 4, 1990, this aircraft and B-47E 51-5251—the last B-47s in storage—were sold to AMCEP Inc. (Bob's Airpark), an aircraft salvage company outside AMARC's perimeter. *Brian Baker*

American political intervention in Vietnam saw the commitment of military forces escalate. To support operations in Southeast Asia, MASDC personnel were busy processing aircraft out of storage for overhaul at depots and subsequent deployment. In early 1966, 33 Douglas C-47s and seven RB-66s were sent to Vietnam—their value when acquired was more than $22 million. To supply the needs of the B-52 fleet, 24 J-57-29 engines were removed from B-52Bs in storage and trucked to March AFB, California, and airlifted to Guam's Anderson Air Base.

To meet the demand for aircraft storage, an additional 600 acres were purchased on the east side of the field. This brought MASDC's total acreage up to 2,822. More than 92,500 man-hours, or 13.6 percent of MASDC's work, was devoted to supporting Vietnam War operations in 1967. For the Navy, 86 A-4s and 74 F-8s were transferred to the overhaul facility at NAS Alameda, California. More B-52 engines—266 worth $56,921,974, and 20 B-66 engines worth

The last of the Navy's piston-powered advanced trainers in storage is T-28C, Bu.No. 146288, which arrived at AMARC on February 21, 1986. The Navy bought 299 T-28Cs and, after production had ceased, converted an additional 72 ex-Air Force T-28As to "C" configuration. The "C" model featured a tail hook, and trained Naval aviators until the type's retirement in 1984. *Nicholas A. Veronico*

Davis-Monthan's storage inventory began with B-29s and C-47s. The majority of the B-29s were gone by 1961, but the C-47 Skytrain was another story. Affectionately known as the "Gooney Bird," the plane saw service in Vietnam, and an era ended on March 2, 1994, when the last Skytrain was sold. 44-76642 was sold to Allied Aircraft Sales of Tucson, and then to Basler Turbo Conversions of Oshkosh, Wisconsin, and was trucked to its new home. This aircraft was delivered to the AAF on March 30, 1945, flew with the 12th Air Force in Italy, and was stateside with the RFC by September 17, 1945. The Skytrain's last operational unit was the 380th Strategic Aerospace Wing and it was retired on November 3, 1969. The last Skytrain was photographed a few months before its departure on July 20, 1993. *Nicholas A. Veronico*

In addition to storing aircraft and missile systems, AMARC also manages production tooling and the occasional battlefield decoy. *Ron Strong*

$4.5 million—were removed from stored aircraft and shipped overseas. The first AGM-28 "Hound Dog" air-launched missiles began arriving for storage during the year.

Meanwhile, 25 B-47s per month were being processed through reclamation. All radar recording cameras, each equipped with two film magazines, were saved for the Environmental Science Services Administration.

Although the end of the Vietnam War was still years in the future, on January 1, 1969, the "Pacer Harvest" plan was released to deal with the anticipated reduction in military forces once hostilities had ceased. To meet immediate demands in Southeast Asia, 99 aircraft were removed from storage for the conflict.[201]

The face of warfare was changing, and the B-58 Hustler was scheduled to be phased out by June 1970. Simultaneously, the U.S. Air Force was developing the Advanced Manned Strategic Aircraft, which became the B-1 bomber, and contracts for its development had been let in June also. Hustler phase-out moved ahead of schedule and all aircraft were at MASDC by January 16, 1970, when 55-662 and 61-0278 arrived from the 305th Bomb Wing. Eighty-four aircraft were in storage, and only two aircraft escaped the smelter. B-58A, 59-2442, was donated to the Pima Air and Space Museum, and TB-58A, 55-0668, eventually ended up at the Lone Star Flight Museum, Galveston, Texas.[202] The remaining Hustlers were sold as a single lot to Southwestern Alloys of Tucson, Arizona, for disposal in 1976.

The mix of aircraft in storage was also changing. When the Army closed the helicopter training base at Fort Wolters, Texas, 90 TH-55As began filling the MASDC ramps—15 per day. In September 1970, 12 railroad cars and 21 trucks brought CGM-13B Mace missiles for storage. From 1966 to 1970, 1,277 aircraft were removed from storage for flight, and 4,495 had been placed into long-term storage. When

Above: The Stratojet was retired from the Air Force's inventory with the last B-47E arriving in February 11, 1966, followed by the last RB-47H on December 29, 1967. America's first swept-wing all-jet bomber fleet covered hundreds of acres at MASDC. *AMARC photo*

Left: A sea of B-52s, on display for easy verification by Russian nuclear arms control experts, bask in the Arizona sun. Has the U.S. destroyed its previously agreed upon number of nuclear bombers? How many in this picture are no longer airworthy? Chopping them into pieces is the only way to be sure. *Nicholas A. Veronico*

700 truckloads of 14,601 bundles of AM-2 temporary runway surface matting arrived for storage from Vietnam, it was requested that 8,681 bundles of the aluminum matting be used to form a 183,000-square-yard parking apron for aircraft returning to flight status. This request was approved and work was begun by Air National Guard personnel in June 1972. The AM-2 matting is still in place to this day.

A number of 1950s-era aircraft were arriving at MASDC in the 1974–75 time frame. Forty-four of the 50 C-133s built ended their days at MASDC. The final C-124 Globemaster from the Air Force's inventory arrived from the 165th Tactical Airlift Command, Georgia Air Guard, in August 1974. Wing spar damage, the high cost of fuel, and a shortage of R-4360 replacement parts all contributed to the grounding of the C-124. The Navy's last C-54, Bu.No. 56501, a C-54Q, arrived for storage from the Naval Test Pilot School, Patuxent River, Maryland, on April 2, 1974. While the propeller-driven

cargo planes were coming in, Air Force C-5As were hauling CH-46A Sky Knights, three per flight, to the rework facility at Cherry Point, North Carolina.

During Davis-Monthan's fourth decade of aircraft storage, many of the Century series fighters were being salvaged. The Pave Deuce project saw 145 F-102As converted into aerial targets as QF-102B drones. In November 1982, F-100s began flying out for drone conversion at Sperry's Litchfield Park facility or Tracor Flight Systems' Mojave, California, operation. In January 1987, F-106As began the drone conversion process, and more than 180 have been converted to date.

In October 1985, MASDC was changed to the Aerospace Maintenance And Regeneration Center (AMARC). The name change was the first step in an effort to inform the American taxpayer of the tremendous value of Davis-Monthan's storage activities, not only in returning millions of dollars' worth of parts and aircraft to the inventory, but to show the

Still in storage at the turn of the century, Lockheed T-1A Seastar, Bu. No. 142263, arrived at Davis-Monthan on April 6, 1970. The Seastar is the Navy's version of the T-33 Shooting Star, modified for carrier operations. The type's first flight was on December 16, 1953, and the aircraft is powered by a 6,000-pound static thrust J33-A-24 engine. *Nicholas A. Veronico*

industrial importance to its southern Arizona neighbors. Unfortunately, in popular culture, when a name sticks, it is hard to change no matter what the benefit to society. AMARC has fought hard to move away from the "boneyard" perception to one of maintenance and regeneration. If the value of storage activities were totaled for the 54 years from 1946 to the year 2000, AMARC and its predecessors have returned or saved the American taxpayer tens of billions of dollars.

AMARC Today

AMARC's mission involves aircraft storage, parts, aircraft withdrawal—both fly away and overland—and storage of nonaircraft items. AMARC provides a managed storage program for aircraft in one of four categories: Type 1000 storage (long term)—these aircraft are stored intact; Type 2000 storage (reclamation)—these planes give up valuable parts and systems to keep other aircraft flying; Type 3000 storage (flyable)—usually a 90-day hold, where an aircraft can be returned to service in a matter of hours; and Type 499 storage—disposal. Flyable storage can be selected for an aircraft, but a decision on the aircraft's storage category is made by the 180th day. Planes awaiting transfer under foreign military sales agreements are often stored this way.

In addition to aircraft, AMARC stores aircraft production tooling for the B-1 and A-10, Titan II missiles, reentry vehicles, photo reconnaissance processing shelters, and communications-electromagnetic-meteorological vans.

Public Tours of AMARC

Tours of AMARC are available for the general public through the Pima Air and Space Museum, 6000 E. Valencia Road, Tucson, Arizona. Air-conditioned tour buses depart the museum's entrance for AMARC five times per day, Monday through Friday, excluding federal holidays. Cameras are allowed on the one-hour narrated tour, and visitors must remain onboard the bus at all times. The bus puts photographers 7 feet off the ground, presenting a unique view of the aircraft in storage. This results in many interesting angles and unique images.

Reservations are recommended, and should be made at least seven days in advance by calling Tel. (520) 618-4806. Everyone over 16 years of age must present photo identification.

In addition to AMARC tours, the Pima Air and Space Museum has acquired one of the most diverse collections of military aircraft—many of which were formerly stored at AMARC. The museum was founded in 1966 by the Air Force Association's Tucson chapter, and in October 1969, 35 aircraft from AMARC's Celebrity Row were transferred to the museum to form the basis of the collection. The museum and its collection of 75 aircraft formally opened to the public on May 8, 1976.

Today there are more than 230 aircraft in the collection that range from World War II–era bombers such as the B-17, B-24, and B-29 to the Century series of fighters—F-101, F-102, F-104, F-105, and F-106, to the VC-118 used by Presidents Kennedy and Johnson, to the supersonic B-58 and SR-71. The museum has a snack bar and well-stocked gift shop. All public areas of the facility are handicapped accessible.

Convair B-58A, 61-2080, was one of two Hustlers to be spared when the fleet was scrapped in the summer of 1977. The supersonic bomber is now on display at the Pima Air and Space Museum.
Nicholas A. Veronico

The Pima Air and Space Museum opened the Titan Missile Museum 25 miles south of Tucson (at 1580 W. Duval Mine Rd., Sahuarita, Arizona) in May 1986. Tours of the former Titan II missile in its underground silo show the complex as it was when operated by the U.S. Air Force's 390th Strategic Missile Wing. Visit the museum's Web site for tour times and prices. Additionally, Pima Air and Space Museum is the site of The Challenger Learning Center of the Southwest, which opened to the public in March 1999.

For a virtual tour of AMARC, visit www.dm.af.mil/AMARC/virtualtour.htm. Additional information, events, and a listing of Pima Air and Space Museum aircraft can be obtained at www.pimaair.org.

The C-124 fleet was retired due to metal fatigue in the wing spars and deliveries of Lockheed's C-141 Starlifter, which could haul greater loads farther than the Globemaster. C-124, serial number 52-1051, awaits the scrapper's blade in May 1971. *Harry Holgerson Jr.*

AMARC has also played a large role in America's compliance with armament reduction treaties. The 1987 Intermediate Range Nuclear Forces Treaty between the United States and the Soviet Union called for the destruction of 443 ground-launched cruise missiles. The project was completed in May 1991.

The death of the B-52 fleet was signaled on July 21, 1991, when the United States and the Soviet Union (now the Commonwealth of Independent States—Belarus, Kazakstan, Russia, and the Ukraine) entered into the Strategic Arms Reduction Treaty (START). The treaty calls for each nation to reduce its nuclear weapons–capable intercontinental and submarine-launched ballistic missiles and strategic bombers to 1,600. To meet this goal, 365 B-52s are being cut into five sections using a 13,000-pound blade dropped from a crane—one cut ahead of the wing root, one behind the trailing edge, and each wing is severed. The broken B-52s are left in orderly piles for 90 days to allow satellite verification of the scrapping by the Commonwealth of Independent States. On December 15, 1994, the final two B-52Ds (56-0672 and 56-0614) fell to the chopping blade. It is now the B-52G's turn. The blade method does not make clean cuts and, in an effort to salvage as much as possible from the remaining B-52Gs, the Commonwealth of Independent States has agreed to allow AMARC to use a plasma saw to surgically cut the bombers into five pieces.

When an aircraft arrives at AMARC, it is assigned a production control number for inventory

The first B-58A, 58-1018, wearing MASDC inventory number BQ026 on the nose gear door, last served with the 43rd Bomb Wing, and arrived for storage on December 15, 1969. Eighty-two B-58s are seen in storage in this 1971 photo. *AMARC photo*

management. The plane then has any armament and ejection seat charges removed, classified items are stored, and a detailed inspection is accomplished. The fuel system is drained and the engine preserved. The hydraulic system is serviced, the aircraft is thoroughly washed and sprayed with a corrosion inhibitor. Then the plane is towed to the shelter area to begin the sealing process. All openings on the upper sides of the aircraft are taped, leaving the lower portion open for air circulation. Engine inlet and exhausts are covered and then the first of two coats of plastic spraylat is applied. The first layer is black, and the top layer is white to reflect sunlight. The combination of open lower areas and spraylat applied to

RP-3A, Bu.No. 149670, arrived at AMARC from the Naval Research Laboratory on May 19, 1994. Two aircraft (149667 and 150500) were designated RP-3As and fitted for oceanographic reconnaissance. Bu.No. 149670 was modified for a different role—electronic reconnaissance for the Naval Research Laboratory—and was also given the same designation. The antenna-sprouting Orion awaits a new mission. *Ron Strong*

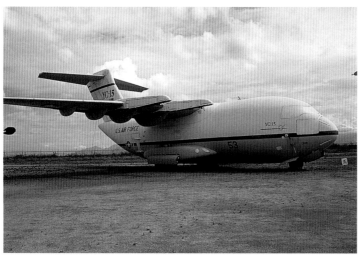

YC-15A, serial number 72-1875, arrived at AMARC on August 20, 1979; the second prototype, 79-1876, followed the next day. The YC-15 and Boeing's YC-14 were designed to meet the Air Force's Advanced Medium Short Takeoff/Landing Transport specification in the early 1970s. Each manufacturer developed a technology demonstration aircraft that featured externally blown flaps using engine exhaust to produce lift, which improved takeoff and landing performance. Neither aircraft was selected for production, although much of the technology was incorporated into today's C-17 Globemaster III. The first YC-15A was displayed at the Pima Air and Space Museum for a number of years and was seen there in July 1993 (left). It was returned to service for additional tests in 1998 (top). *Terry Vanden Heuvel (top) and Nicholas A. Veronico (left)*

canopies and upper surfaces allows an aircraft's interior to maintain a temperature within 15 to 20 degrees of the outside air temperature. Every six months after arrival, aircraft are inspected to ensure that the elements have not damaged the spraylat and, after four years, the planes are recycled through the preservation process.

Aircraft depart AMARC in one of two ways—under their own power or on a truck. Over the years, it has been estimated that more than 25 percent of all aircraft in storage have flown out for further service. AMARC technicians prepare the aircraft for flight by withdrawing the plane from storage, inspecting and repairing or overhauling systems, and modifying an aircraft to current standards by meeting Time Compliance Technical Orders. Many aircraft or subassemblies such as nose sections or fuselages slated for use as trainers are

AMARC strives to recover every item possible from an aircraft to provide the greatest return for every taxpayer dollar spent. Boeing EC-135G, serial number 62-3570, demonstrates AMARC's ability to use every piece of an aircraft's carcass. This former SAC airborne launch control center and radio relay aircraft began life weighing in at more than 98,000 pounds. As it sits today, it has been reduced to two tons of recyclable aluminum.
Nicholas A. Veronico

trucked from the center. Currently, a large number of F-4s are being readied for flight to contractors for drone conversion as part of the Air Combat Command's Full Scale Aerial Target Program.

Aircraft in Type 2000 storage have been slated for reclamation to provide a source of spare parts to maintain the air forces of our military. Priority removal of parts is accomplished to meet the demand for parts or assemblies that cannot be obtained from normal supply channels. Programmed reclamation meets the long-term supply needs for various aircraft programs. Parts are cleaned, tested, packaged, and shipped to repair depots around the world.[203]

To commemorate the sacrifices of this nation's service men and women, obsolete combat aircraft and missiles are made available as loans or gifts to museums, qualifying municipalities, or veterans' groups such as the American Legion, Veterans of Foreign Wars, and Disabled American Veterans. AMARC supervises this program by monitoring aircraft loan requests, verifying donation eligibility, and monitoring the removal of aircraft from storage.[204] Donation aircraft are offered on an "as-is, where-is" basis, and each receiving organization must bear the full cost to disassemble, transport, and display an aircraft within 90 days. Once an aircraft has been placed on display, a yearly photographic survey is made to ensure it is being maintained properly and protected from vandalism and decay.

AMARC is a vital link in America's national defense. At the turn of the century, the center was managing nearly 4,800 aircraft for the Air Force, Army, Navy, and Coast Guard. As defense budgets are tightened and fewer new aircraft are acquired, the United States and allied nations will increase demands on AMARC's services.

APPENDICES

Appendix I
Reconstruction Finance Corporation Sales and Storage Fields, September 1945
(Cities listed alphabetically by states.)

Location	Airport	Location	Airport
Birmingham, Alabama	Municipal	Omaha, Nebraska	Municipal
Phoenix, Arizona	Thunderbird II	Reno, Nevada	Reno
Tucson, Arizona	Ryan	Readington, New Jersey	Solberg-Hunterton
Wickenburg, Arizona	Echeverria	Albuquerque, New Mexico	Army Air Field
Pine Bluff, Arkansas	Grider	Albany, New York	Albany
West Helena, Arkansas	Thompson-Robbins	Rochester, New York	Municipal
Blythe, California	Gary	White Plains, New York	Westchester County
Concord, California	Sherman	Charlotte, North Carolina	Cannon
Fresno, California	Chandler Field	Akron, Ohio	Municipal
Hemet, California	Ryan	Cincinnati, Ohio	Lunkin
Ontario, California	Cal-Aero	Muskogee, Oklahoma	Hat Box
Denver, Colorado	Rutledge	Oklahoma City, Oklahoma	Cimarron
Miami, Florida	Chapman	Ponca City, Oklahoma	Municipal
St. Petersburg, Florida	Ludwig-Sky Harbor	Portland, Oregon	Portland-Troutdale
Americus, Georgia	Souther	Pittsburgh, Pennsylvania	Bettis
Augusta, Georgia	Bush	Bennettsville, South Carolina	Palmer
Douglas, Georgia	Municipal	Camden, South Carolina	Woodward
Lansing, Illinois	Ford-Lansing	Sioux Falls, South Dakota	Sioux
Indianapolis, Indiana	Sky Harbor	Jackson, Tennessee	McKellar
Davenport, Iowa	Cran	Union City, Tennessee	Embry-Riddle
Wichita, Kansas	Municipal	Ballinger, Texas	Bruce
Baton Rouge, Louisiana	E. Baton Rouge Parish	Corsicana, Texas	Corsicana
North Grafton, Massachusetts	North Grafton	Cuero, Texas	Municipal
Lansing, Michigan	Capitol City	Fort Stockton, Texas	Gibbs
Minneapolis, Minnesota	Victory	Fort Worth, Texas	Hicks
Clarksdale, Mississippi	Fletcher	Houston, Texas	Municipal
Madison, Mississippi	Augustine	Lamesa, Texas	Lamesa
Cape Girardeau, Missouri	Harris	San Antonio, Texas	Municipal
Kansas City, Missouri	Municipal	Stamford, Texas	Arledge
Robertson, Missouri	Municipal	Vernon, Texas	Victory
Sikeston, Missouri	Harvey Park	Salt Lake City, Utah	Municipal No. 1
Helena, Montana	Municipal	Alexandria, Virginia	Hybia Valley
		Morgantown, West Virginia	Municipal

Appendix II

Distribution of Aircraft Inventory by Location, June 27, 1946

Location of Aircraft	Total Number	Percent of Total
Albuquerque, New Mexico	1,706	5.0
Altus, Oklahoma	2,543	7.5
Augusta, Georgia	989	2.9
Ballinger, Texas	305	0.9
Blythe, California	373	1.1
Camden, South Carolina	786	2.3
Cape Girardeau, Missouri	110	0.3
Clinton, Oklahoma	8,028	23.6
Cuero, Texas	423	1.2
Decatur, Alabama	215	0.6
Dos Palos, California	126	0.4
Ft. Worth, Texas	431	1.3
Harvey Point, N. Carolina	97	0.3
Jackson, Tennessee	402	1.2
Kingman, Arizona	5,553	16.3
Lamesa, Texas	325	1.0
Madison, Mississippi	338	1.0
Muskogee, Oklahoma	117	0.3
Oklahoma City, Oklahoma	945	2.8
Ontario, California	1,879	5.5
Phoenix, Arizona	28	0.1
Pine Bluff, Arkansas	140	0.4
Ponca City, Oklahoma	165	0.5
Stamford, Texas	242	0.7
Union City, Tennessee	596	1.8
Vernon, Texas	1,322	3.9
Walnut Ridge, Arkansas	5,660	16.7
Wickenburg, Arizona	138	0.4
Total	33,982	100.0

Source: War Assets Administration, Monthly Progress Report, June 1946

Appendix III

Limited-Type Certificates (LTC) Issued by the CAA for Surplus Military Aircraft
Compiled by William T. Larkins

LTC	Issued	Aircraft type	Original TC Holder
1	12/02/46	B-17F, G	TWA
2	12/06/46	RB-25, B-25C	Shell Aviation Corp.
3	12/19/46	A-26B, A-26C	Paul V. Shields
4	01/09/47	A-24B, SBD-5	Seaboard & Western
5	02/19/47	PB2Y-3, 3R PB2Y-5, 5R, 5Z	Robert M. Lewis
6	02/21/47	LB-30	Convair
7	02/28/47	R-4B	Douglas W. Holmes
8	03/17/47	TBF-1, 1C TBM-3, 3E	Air Trading Corp.
9	03/31/47	A-20B, C, G, H, J	Hughes Aircraft Corp.
10	04/07/47	P-38E, J, L, M F-5E, F, G	Lockheed Aircraft Corp.
11	04/10/47	P-51C, D, K	DiPonti Aviation Co.
12	04/14/47	AT-10	Leland H. Cameron
13	04/15/47	B-34, PV-1, PV-2	Air Trading Corp.
14	04/23/47	P-61, A, B	Northrop Aircraft Inc.
15	04/30/47	A-36A	Woodrow W. Edmondson
16	05/06/47	O-52	Holmberg Aerial Survey
17	05/06/47	J2F-3, 4, 5, 6	R. B. Utterback
18	05/08/47	P-40L, N	Boardman C. Reed
19	05/15/47	R-5A	Hel-I-Corp Advertising
20	06/06/47	PBM-5	Carl F. Krogman
21	07/17/47	P-63C, E	Bell Aircraft Corp.
22	08/08/47	BC-1	Mustang Aviation Inc.
23	08/29/47	F8F-1	Grumman
24	10/08/47	OS2U-1, 2, 3 OS2N-1	Carl F. Krogman
25	11/05/47	FM-2	Richard R. Carlisle
26	11/17/47	L-1, A, B, C, D L-1E, F	Executive Airlines
27	11/18/47	BT-9, A, B, C	James O. Wyatt
28	12/16/47	PQ-14A, B YPQ-14A, B TD2C-1	N. A. Kalt
29	01/05/48	YR-6A, R-6A HOS-1	Stolp-Adams Co.
30	01/06/48	C-87A	William P. Odom
31	01/14/48	AT-9, AT-9A	L. S. Rehr
32	01/14/48	BT-14	P. J. Franklin

Appendix IV

Larkins' Kingman Photograph Tables

Table One
8th Air Force B-17s Identified In Larkins' Kingman Photos

Tail Letter	Squadron Letters/Numbers	Group, Squadron	AAF Serial
Triangle A	OR-M	91BG, 323 BS	
Triangle A	LG-U	91BG, 322 BS	44-6591
Triangle A	OR-B	91 BG, 323 BS	42-32116
Square A	-R	94 BG	43-38897
Square A	-W	94 BG	44-8745
Square B	-B	95 BG	44-6134
Square B	-T	95 BG	43-38996
Square B	-U	95 BG	44-8529
Square B	ET-G	95 BG, 336 BS	
Triangle C	VK-	303 BG, 358 BS	
Triangle C	PU-C	303 BG, 360 BS	43-38608
Square C	S-H	96 BG	43-37623
Square C	-H	96BG	43-37716
Square C	-S	96BG	
Square C	QJ-M	96 BG, 339 BS	
Square D	XR-	100 BG, 349 BS	
Square D	-B	100 BG	42-37972
Triangle G	-H	305 BG	44-6015
Triangle G	JJ-Q	305 BG, 422 BS	
Square H	-H	388 BG	43-39309
Square H	-M	388 BG	43-33229
Triangle J	-Y	351 BG	
Triangle J	YB-K	351 BG, 508 BS	
Triangle J	YB-L	351 BG, 508 BS	
Square J	-P	390 BG	44-8206
Square J	BI-Q	390 BG, 568 BS	43-38724
Square J	BI-B	390 BG, 568 BS	
Square J	CC-P	390 BG, 569 BS	
Square J	DI-I	390 BG, 580 BS	44-6906
Square J	-J	390 BG	43-38328
Square K	-D	447 BG	42-97976
Square K	-G	447 BG	42-31225
Square K	-M	447 BG	44-8310
Square K	-P	447 BG	
Square K	-U	447 BG	44-8415
Triangle L	VE-O	381 BG, 532 BS	42-10711
Square L	+5	452 BG	
Square L	KG-G+	452 BG	44-6827
M with Checkers	385 BG	42-38031	
Triangle P	BK-A	834 BG, 546 BS	42-97510
Square P	2G-E	487 BG, 836 BS	43-39249
Square P	2G-G	487 BG, 836 BS	
Square P	4F-	487 BG, 837 BS	44-6315
Square P	R5-I	487 BG, 839 BS	
Square P	R5-H	487 BG, 839 BS	
Triangle S	IN-R	401 BG, 613 BS	
Triangle S	IW-N	401 BG, 614 BS	43-38738
Triangle U	AL-N	457 BG	42-97123
Triangle W	30-L	398 BG, 601 BS	
Square W	-----	486 BG	43-37968

Table Two
15th Air Force B-17s at Kingman

Markings	Number	Group	Serial Number
Y in circle	2	2 BG	44-6545
Y in circle	2	2 BG	44-6850
Y in triangle		97 BG	44-8114
Y in diamond		99 BG	44-6376

Table Three
Combat B-24s Identified from Photos Taken at Kingman

Tail Marking	Bomb Group	Air Force
Diagonal bar & rudder stripes	43rd	5th
Skull and crossed bombs	90th	5th
Solid triangle	11 BO, 26 BS	7th
Solid square	11 BG, 42 BS	7th
Horizontal V	494 BG, 864 BS	7th
Diagonal bar	494 BG, 865 BS	7th
Two vertical bars	494 BG, 866 BS	7th
Colored quarters	494 BG, 867 BS	7th
Vertical stripe & underline	44th	8th
Vertical stripe	389th	8th
Horizontal stripe	392nd	8th
Horizontal stripe	446th	8th
Diagonal band	448th	8th
Diagonal band	492nd	8th
LR	307th	13th
S in diamond	868 BS	13th
Diamond and checkers	459th	15th
Square and vertical bar	464th	15th
Square and two bars	465th	15th
"Bow tie" X and colors	484th	15th
X and rectangle	485th	15th

BIBLIOGRAPHY

Books

Andrade, John M. *U.S. Military Aircraft Designations and Serials Since 1909.* Earl Shilton, Leicestershire, England: Midland Counties Publications, 1979.

Andrews, Paul M., and William H. Adams. *Heavy Bombers of the Mighty Eighth.* Savannah, Ga.: Eighth Air Force Memorial Museum Foundation, 1995.

Birdsall, Steve. *Log of the Liberators.* Garden City, N.Y.: Doubleday & Company, Inc., 1973.

Blanchard, Peter, Philip Chinnery, and Martyn Swann. *MASDC: Military Aircraft Storage & Disposition Center.* London: Aviation Press Ltd., 1983.

Chinnery, Philip. *Desert Boneyard.* Airlife England. 1987.

Chinnery, Philip D. *50 Years of the Desert Boneyard.* Osceola, Wis.: MBI Publishing Company, 1995.

Freeman, Roger A. *B-17 Fortress at War.* New York: Charles Scribner's Sons, 1977.

Grantham, A. Kevin. *P-Screamers: The History of the Surviving Lockheed P-38 Lightnings.* Missoula, Mont.: Pictorial Histories Publishing Company, 1994.

Havener, J. K. *The Martin B-26 Marauder.* Blue Ridge Summit, Penn.: Aero, 1988.

Johnson, Dave. *The Aerospace Maintenance And Regeneration Center.* West Drayton, Middlesex, England: LAAS International, 1995.

Knaack, Marcelle S. *Encyclopedia of U.S. Air Force Aircraft and Missile Systems: Post-World War II Bombers*: Washington, D.C.: Office of Air Force History, 1988.

Miller, Jay. *Convair B-58 Hustler: The World's First Supersonic Bomber.* Earl Shilton, Leicestershire., England: Aerofax/Midland Publishing Ltd., 1997.

Mitchell, S., and A. Eastwood. *Military Aircraft Serials of North America.* West Drayton, Middlesex, England: The Aviation Hobby Shop, 1991.

Mueller, Robert. *Air Force Bases, Volume 1.* Washington, D.C.: Office of Air Force History, 1989.

Pratt, Joseph A., and Christopher J. Castaneda. *Builders: Herman and George Brown.* College Station: Texas A&M University Press, 1999.

Railing, Lawrence C. *Profile History: Military Aircraft Storage and Disposition Center and Predecessor Organizations, 1946-1974.* Davis-Monthan Air Force Base, Arizona: Air Force Logistics Command, 1975.

Shettle, Mel. *United States Naval Air Stations of World War II, Volume 2: Western States.* Bowersville, Ga.: Schaertel Publishing Company, 1997.

Thompson, Scott. *B-25 Mitchell in Civil Service.* Elk Grove, Calif.: Aero Vintage Books, 1997.

Thompson, Scott. *Final Cut: The Post-War B-17 Flying Fortress.* Missoula, Mont.: Pictorial Histories Publishing Company, 1990.

Veronico, Nicholas A., and Marga Fritze. *Blue Angels: Fifty Years of Precision Flight.* Osceola, Wis: MBI Publishing Company, 1996.

Veronico, Nicholas A. *F4U Corsair: The Combat, Development, and Racing History of the Corsair.* Osceola, Wis.: MBI Publishing Company, 1994.

Veronico, Nicholas A., and Jim Dunn. *Giant Cargo Planes.* Osceola, Wis.: MBI Publishing Company,1999.

Periodicals

Armstrong, William J. "Letter to the Editor (Clinton, OK)," *The Hook,* Spring 1983.

Baker, Brian. "Surplus Aircraft at Litchfield Park," *Journal of the American Aviation Historical Society,* AAHS, April–June 1958, 131–32.

Birdsall, Steve. "Arizona Sundown," *Air Classics,* December 1969, pp. 14–21.

Bowers, Peter M. "The Saga of 5-Grand," *Wings,* June 1978, pp.10–19.

Brinkley, Floyd. "White Elephants for Sale," *Air Force Magazine,* September 1946.

Cooper, Tom C. "Where B-52s Come Home to Roost," *Seattle Times Magazine,* September 19, 1971, pp. 8–10.

Dennison, Robert C. "Stratojet Swan Song," *Military Surplus Warplanes,* Fall 1997, pp. 50–55.

Farmer, James H. "Saga of the Civil Forts; Part 1—The Era of the WAA and the Years of Plenty," *Journal of the American Aviation Historical Society,* AAHS, Winter 1977, pp. 292–302.

Kelly, Leo. "Altus Air Force Base: Sentinel of Southwest Oklahoma," *The Chronicles of Oklahoma,* The Oklahoma Historical Society, Fall 1997.

Kroger, William. "Junking of Old Planes Pressed Before 'Economy' Clamor Rises," *Aviation News,* November 26, 1945, pp. 13, 14.

Larkins, William T. "Kingman, Arizona-1947: A Personal View," *Aerophile*, June 1979, pp. 16–25.

_____. "War Album," *The Aeroplane Spotter*, June 14, 1947, p. 128.

_____. "Forgotten Warbird Graveyard," *Air Classics Quarterly Review*, Winter 1978, pp. 44–57.

_____. "War Assets: Part One," *Air Classics*, February 1992, p. 17.

_____. "War Assets: Part Two," *Air Classics*, March 1992, p. 13.

_____. "War Assets: Part Three," *Air Classics*, April 1992, p. 16.

_____. "Return to Kingman," *Air Classics*, May 1997, pp. 22–33.

McLain, Jerry. "Warbirds' Swansong," *Arizona Highways*, May 1947, p. 1.

Miller, J. J., and Guy Patterson. "Death of an Air Force," *Flying*, November 1947, pp. 22–33.

Moll, Nigel. "Ghost Story," *Flying*, February 1989, pp. 65–75.

Montagnes, James. "Salvaging Our Surplus Warplanes —In Canada," *Flying*, September 1945, p. 44.

O'Leary, Michael, and Milo Peltzer. "Return to Kingman," *Air Classics*, May 1997, pp. 22, 23.

Peck, Phillips J. "Salvaging Our Surplus Warplanes— In the U.S.," *Flying*, September 1945, p. 45.

Peltzer, Milo, and Michael O'Leary. "Ghosts of Litchfield Park," *Military Surplus Warplanes,* Fall 1997, pp. 4–21.

Schirmer, Col. Frank. "History of the 4105th AAF Base Unit, 1945–1948," *Journal of the American Aviation Historical Society*, AAHS, Spring 1986, pp. 12–25.

Sherman, Gene. "Warplanes Go to Arizona Desert to Die," *Los Angeles Times*, April 1, 1946, p. 1.

Thompson, Scott. "Postwar Aircraft Disposal," *Journal of the American Aviation Historical Society*, AAHS, Winter 1992, pp. 274–87.

Unknown. "Planes Go Begging," *Business Week,* April 4, 1945, p. 108.

_____. "Surplus Warplanes Jam RFC Depots," *Aviation News*, August 6, 1945, p. 20.

_____. "Larger Dealer Role in Disposal of Surplus PTs Appears Justified," *Aviation News,* December 3, 1945, p. 15.

_____. "U.S. Surplus Aircraft Abroad Sell Slowly," *Aviation News*, December 2, 1945, p. 15.

_____. "Consolidated-Vultee Basic Trainers for Sale by RFC at $975," *Aviation News*, January 28, 1946, p. 41.

_____. "Terrors Last Year—Junk Today," *Aviation News,* April 8, 1946, p. 7.

_____. "Death in the Desert," *Business Week,* April 13, 1946, p. 21.

_____. "WAA Lists Sales of Surplus Planes," *Aviation News*, May 27, 1946, p. 9.

_____. "Surplus Transport Sales," *Aviation News*, September 9, 1946, p. 11.

_____. "1,522 Surplus Planes Still Held by FLC (Foreign Liquidations Commissioner)," *Aviation News*, December 2, 1946, p. 9.

_____. "Trainer Price Cut," *Aviation News*, December 2, 1946, p. 9.

_____. "Clippers for Sale, $50,000 Each While They Last as Surplus," *Flying,* August 1946, pp. 50, 51.

_____. "Where Are They Now?" *The Aeroplane Spotter*, June 14, 1947, pp. 126, 127.

_____. "Acres of Aircraft," *Naval Aviation News*, April 1948, p. 120.

_____. "Navy Guillotine Chops Up Planes for Salvage," *Naval Aviation News*, April 1948, p. 25.

_____. "Storage Merged for USAF-Navy Aircraft," *Naval Aviation News*, July 1966, p. 18, 19.

_____. "Smelter Skelter ...," *EAA Warbirds*, July 1990.

_____. "2,500,000 Gals. Gas 'Sold Twice' by U.S.," *The New York Times*. Thursday, August 22, 1946, p. 1.

Government Documents

_____. *Aircraft and Aircraft Parts*, Report of the Surplus Property Administration to the Congress, November 23, 1945.

_____. *Aircraft and Components—1946,* Report No. 470-W-4 by the Progress Analysis Division, WAA, Washington, D.C.

_____. *Army Air Forces Statistical Digest*, (AAF) Office of Statistical Control, December 1945.

_____. *Disposal of Surplus Aircraft and Major Components Thereof,* Harvard University, May 22, 1945 (and reported to the Congressional Committee on Military Affairs, June 26, 1944).

_____. *How to Buy Surplus Aircraft, Parts, and Miscellaneous Air Equipment*, Office of Aircraft Disposal, WAA, Washington, D.C., 1946.

_____. *How to Do Business with the RFC,* Reconstruction Finance Corporation, August 1945.

_____. *Monthly Progress Report*, WAA, June 1946.

_____. *Quarterly Reports* to the Congress by the Reconstruction Finance Corporation for 1945.

_____. *Quarterly Reports* to the Congress by the War Assets Administration for 1946 and 1947.

_____. *RFC Surplus Property News*, various, but especially August 1945, November 1945, and December 1945.

_____. *Sale of Aircraft, Kingman, Arizona,* Subcommittee of the Committee on Expenditures in the Executive Department, U.S. Senate, June 4, 18–19, 1947.

_____. *Minutes of Aircraft Review Board*, June 13, 1947.

_____. *United States Naval Aviation 1910–1980*, Department of the Navy, 1981.

_____. "Modern Electric Guillotine Speeds Salvage of Aluminum from Obsolete Navy Planes," U.S. Navy Press Release, NAS Norfolk, April 4, 1948.

_____. *War Assets Administration Surplus Property News*, various, but especially March 1946.

_____. *War Wings for Peace*, Division of Information, War Assets Administration, 1946.

_____. *White Elephants With Wings*, Office of Surplus Property, undated.

_____. "RFC Surplus Government Property, Aircraft, For Sale." Pamphlet, September 6, 1945.

Trester, Dorothy W. *History of the AF Storage and Withdrawal Program* (1945–1952), Historical Division, Office of Information Services, Air Materiel Command, Wright-Patterson AFB, Ohio, 1954 (available on USAF HRC microfilm reel #K2018).

AAF Technical Order No. 00-25-30. "Miscellaneous—Unit Costs of Aircraft and Engines." August 1, 1945.

War Assets Administration Advance Releases

No. 853, December 11, 1946—Sale of 35 Beech GB-2s.

No. 868, December 16, 1946—Sale of R4Ds and R5Ds, etc.

No. 978, January 20, 1947—Sale of 217 BT-13s and 22 AT-19s.

No. 1011, February 1, 1947—Sale of 506 C-46s at Walnut Ridge, 38 at Ontario, and one at Altus, Oklahoma. Average Price $12,500.

No. 1021, February 4, 1947—Lists totals of 31,198 surplus aircraft.

No. 1022, February 4, 1947—Sale of 37 Douglas C-47s.

No. 1079, February 17, 1947—Locations and prices for J4F-1s, JRF-6Bs, etc.

No. 1112, March 3, 1947—Review of 172 aircraft sold.

No. 1241, April 24, 1947—Review of 585 aircraft, types, and locations.

No. 1344, June 6, 1947—Sale of XF2G-1 and other Navy types.

No. 1369, June 27, 1947—Sale of 65,000 aircraft nearly complete.

No. 1399, July 22, 1947—Maj. Gen. Littlejohn reports that 28,900 combat aircraft were disposed of as salvage at an average price of one and one-half cents per pound.

Individual Aircraft Histories

FAA Records, P-51D, NX79111.
FAA Records, P-38F, N5101N.
FAA Records, P-38L, N66613.
FAA Records, P-47M, N27385.

Interviews

Interview, Steve Beville, 1994, 1998, and 1999.
Interview, Bill Lear, 1994.
Interview, Edward Maloney, 1999.
Interview, Julian Q. Myers, 1990 and 1999.
Interview, Fred Nimz, 1991.
Interview, Bill North, 1999.
Interview, J. D. Reed, 1986.
Interview, Lindsey S. Youngblood, 1990, 1994, and 1999.

NOTES

[1] "The Liquidation of War Surpluses," Quarterly Report to the Congress by the Surplus Property Administration, Fourth Quarter 1945, p. 28.

[2] "Army Air Forces Statistical Digest," (AAF) Office of Statistical Control, December 1945, Table 84, and *United States Naval Aviation 1910-1980*, Department of the Navy, 1981, p. 382.

[3] "Surplus Property," Quarterly Report to the Congress by the Surplus Property Administration, Second Quarter 1945, p. 71.

[4] "Aircraft and Aircraft Parts," Report of the Surplus Property Administration to the Congress, November 23, 1945, p. 6.

[5] *The Army Air Forces in World War II*, Volume XII, p. 571.

[6] "History of the U.S. Naval Air Facility, Litchfield Park," as provided by the Naval Historical Center, p. 1.

[7] "The Liquidation of War Surpluses," p. 29.

[8] Ibid.

[9] Numbers based on available information derived from quarterly reports of the WAA to the Congress.

[10] "War Surplus in the Peacetime Economy," Quarterly Report of the WAA, Second Quarter, 1947, p. 11.

[11] "White Elephants With Wings," Office of the Surplus Property Board, undated but available December 1945, p. 16.

[12] "Disposal of Surplus Aircraft and Major Components Thereof," as prepared by Harvard University, May 22, 1945, and reported to the Congressional Committee on Military Affairs, June 26, 1944, p. 87.

[13] "The Aviation Annual of 1946," p. 92.

[14] "White Elephants With Wings," p. 16.

[15] "Disposal of Surplus Aircraft and Major Components Thereof," pp. 82–83.

[16] "Aircraft and Aircraft Parts," p. 5.

[17] "Disposal of Surplus Aircraft and Major Components Thereof," pp. 5–6.

[18] "White Elephants," pp. 16–17.

[19] Ibid.

[20] Ibid.

[21] Ibid., pp. 6–7.

[22] "Aircraft and Aircraft Parts," p. 10.

[23] Numbers approximated from quarterly reports of the WAA.

[24] "Aircraft and Aircraft Parts," pp. 11–13

[25] Ibid.

[26] Ibid.

[27] Ibid.

[28] Ibid.

[29] Ibid., p. 14.

[30] Ibid., p. 13.

[31] Ibid., p. 14.

[32] Ibid.

[33] "White Elephants," p. 12.

[34] Ibid., p. 29.

[35] "Defense Plants Corporation Takes Over Disposal of Airplanes Declared Surplus," *Civil Aeronautics Journal*, December 15, 1944, p. 139.

[36] Ibid.

[37] "Surplus Property," p. 1.

[38] Ibid., p. 17.

[39] "SPB Regulation No. 1" as published in Federal Register, Volume 10, p. 3,764, May 1, 1945.

[40] "The Integration of Surplus Disposal," Quarterly Progress Report to the Congress by the War Assets Administration, First Quarter 1946, p. 6. The WAC was originally created as the Petroleum Reserve Corporation as a subsidiary of the RFC and was renamed the War Assets Corporation on November 15, 1945.

[41] Summary of Harvard and Pogue Reports as provided by the National Archives.

[42] "United States Government Manual," 1946, pp. 75–76.

[43] "United States Government Manual," 1946, p. 620.

[44] "How to Do Business with the RFC," Reconstruction Finance Corporation, August 1945, pp. 31–32.

[45] "Aircraft and Aircraft Parts," p. 23.

[46] "How to Buy an Airplane," *Air Force Magazine*, November 1946, p. 22.

[47] Ibid.

[48] Ibid.

[49] "Aircraft and Aircraft Parts," p. 16.

[50] Ibid., p. 17.

[51] "Quarterly Report," War Assets Administration, 2nd Quarter 1947, p. 11.

[52] "RFC Surplus Property News," Reconstruction Finance Corporation, November 1945, p. 6.

[53] "Surplus Property Regulation 4" as published in the Federal Register, Volume 11, p. 179 (December 21, 1945).

[54] "Sale of Aircraft, Kingman, Arizona," p. 52.

[55] Mohave Museum of History and Arts, http://www/ctaz.com/~mocohist/musuem/home1.html

[56] Julian Myers, interview, 1990.

[57] Ibid.

[58] Ibid.

[59] Ibid.

[60] Jerry McLain, "Warbirds' Swansong," *Arizona Highways*, May 1947, p. 39.

[61] Myers interview.

[62] Ibid.

[63] Ibid.

[64] Ibid.

[65] *P-Screamers, The History of the Surviving Lockheed P-38 Lightnings,* p. 99.

66 Myers interview.

67 "Warbirds' Swansong."

68 Myers interview.

69 "B-17 Fortress at War," p. 183.

70 Mohave Museum of History and Arts.

71 Bill Lear, interview, 1994.

72 *P-Screamers.*

73 Lear interview.

74 "Sale of Aircraft , Kingman, Arizona," p. 5.

75 Ibid., p. 13.

76 Ibid., p. 18.

77 Ibid., p. 23.

78 Ibid., p. 85.

79 Lindsey S. Youngblood, Interview, 1999.

80 "Sale of Aircraft, Kingman, Arizona," p. 11.

81 *Builders,* p. 100.

82 "Sale of Aircraft , Kingman, Arizona," p. 95.

83 Ibid., p. 2.

84 Youngblood interview.

85 Bill North, interview, 1999.

86 Ibid.

87 Youngblood interview.

88 "Sale of Aircraft, Kingman, Arizona," p. 10.

89 Ibid., p. 6.

90 Ibid., p. 9.

91 Ibid., p. 4.

92 Youngblood interview.

93 Myers interview.

94 "Sale of Aircraft, Kingman, Arizona," pp. 50-51.

95 Ibid.

96 Myers interview.

97 "Sale of Aircraft, Kingman, Arizona," p. 55.

98 Ibid., p. 2.

99 Ibid., p. 55.

100 Youngblood interview.

101 "Warbirds' Swansong."

102 Fred Nimz interview, 1991.

103 *Log of the Liberators,* p. 63.

104 Mohave Museum of History and Arts.

105 Ibid.

106 *United States Naval Air Stations of World War II,* Volume 2, p. 43.

107 "RFC to Take Over Stillwater's North Airport as Storage Depot for U.S. Army's War Planes," *Stillwater Daily News-Press,* May 31, 1945.

108 "Quartet of Thunderbolts Land at North City Airport," *Stillwater Gazette,* June 24, 1945.

109 "Quarterly Report of the War Assets Administration," 1st Quarter, 1946, p. 12.

110 Bill of Sale executed between Paul Mantz and the WAC as recorded in the FAA registration files for B-17 N67974.

111 Partnership agreement between Mantz, Hapgood, and Heath, as recorded in the FAA registration files for P-51 N1202.

112 Dwiggins, Don. *Hollywood Pilot: The Biography of Paul Mantz.* New York, Doubleday & Co., 1967, pp. 185–87.

113 "Formal Demand Is Made for Return Of Airport," *Stillwater Gazette,* December 20, 1946.

114 *The Martin B-26 Marauder,* J. K. Havener, p. 244.

115 J. D. Reed, interview, 1989.

116 WAA Bill of Sale Document, P-51D, NX79111.

117 Steve Beville, interview, 1992.

118 FAA records for P-51D, NX79111.

119 Walnut Ridge, Release of Custody of Aircraft Document.

120 Ibid.

121 "Sale of Aircraft, Kingman, Arizona," p. 57.

122 *Builders,* pp. 100, 101.

123 FAA records for P-47M, N27385.

124 FAA records for P-38F, N5101N.

125 Ibid.

126 FAA records for P-47M, N27385.

127 "Sale of Aircarft, Kingman, Arizona," p. 44.

128 *Builders,* pp. 100, 101.

129 "Sale of Aircraft, Kingman, Arizona," p. 46.

130 Ibid.

131 Ibid.

132 *The Martin B-26 Marauder,* J. K. Havener, p. 244.

133 Larkins. "War Assets, Part Two," *Air Classics,* March 1992, p. 21.

134 *Builders,* pp. 100–101.

135 Youngblood interview, 1991.

136 *Builders,* pp. 100–101.

137 Myers interview, 1990.

138 Larkins. "War Assets, Part Two," *Air Classics,* March 1992, p. 21.

139 "Air Force Bases," pp. 287–93.

140 http://www.kirtland.af.mil/history/History.html and http://cted.inel.gov/cted/latest_happenings/history_816.html

141 "Altus Air Force Base: Sentinel of Southwest Oklahoma," *Chronicles of Oklahoma,* pp. 306–19.

142 Ibid.

143 "History of the AF Storage and Withdrawal Program (1945–1952)," p. 15.

144 Ibid., p. 16.

145 "Graveyard for the Eagles," *The Daily Oklahoma,* February 10, 1946.

146 Example of the advertisement can be seen on page 8 of the *New York Times,* April 26, 1947.

147 Details as indicated in the CAA registration records for B-17G N5017N, N5110N, N5111N, and N5116N.

148 Details as indicated in the CAA registration records for B-17G N5017N, N5110N, N5111N, and N5116N.

149 Records between the U.S. Navy and Texas Railway Equipment Corporation as contained in Record Group 72 at the National Archives.

150 "Altus Air Force Base: Sentinel of Southwest Oklahoma," pp. 306–19.

151 "Air Force Bases," p. 2.

152 *United States Naval Air Stations of World War II, Volume 2,* p. 43.

153 Ibid.

154 Letter to the Editor, *The Hook,* Spring 1983, p. 67.

155 "Sale of Aircraft, Kingman, Arizona," p. 52. Note that the WAA's Monthly Progress Report, Section 1A (June 1946)—which is reproduced in Appendix II—shows the total number of aircraft at Clinton as 8,028.

156 "Sale of Aircraft, Kingman, Arizona," pp. 43–47.

157 *B-25 Mitchell in Civil Service.* These three B-25s were N5126N (44-30975), N5856V (44-31104), and N5857V (44-30982).

158 *Naval Air Stations of World War II*, p. 129.

159 "History of the U.S. Naval Air Facility, Litchfield Park," as provided by the Naval Historical Center.

160 *United States Navy and Marine Corps Bases, Domestic*, p. 285.

161 "History of the U.S. Naval Air Facility, Litchfield Park," p. 1.

162 Brian Baker, "Surplus Aircraft at Litchfield Park," *AAHS Journal*, p. 131.

163 "History of the U.S. Naval Air Facility, Litchfield Park," p. 2, *Blue Angels: Fifty Years of Precision Flight*, p. 62.

164 Brian Baker, "Surplus Aircraft at Litchfield Park," *AAHS Journal*, p. 131.

165 *United States Navy and Marine Corps Bases, Domestic*, p. 286.

166 Technical Order 00-25-54, May 25, 1944.

167 "Aircraft Storage Workload, Post V-J Day," memo from Maintenance Control Section, HQ ATSC to Chief, Maintenance Division, HQ ATSC. August 22, 1945.

168 Dorothy W. Trester, *History of the AF Storage and Withdrawl Program, 1945–1952.* Historical Division, Office of Information Services, Air Material Command, Wright Patterson Air Force Base, April 1954, p. 9.

169 The Army Air Forces officially separated from the U.S. Army, becoming the U.S. Air Force on September 18, 1947. Army Air Fields were subsequently renamed Air Force Bases (AFB).

170 Trester, *History of the AF Storage*, p. 26

171 Ibid, p. 26.

172 Ibid, p. 28.

173 Ibid, p. 21.

174 Trester, The Hass contract called for 166 Warner Robins and 97 Ogden, Utah, B-29s to be preserved at a cost of $1,415 each; and 101 at Sacramento, $1,380 each. Fort Pitt's contract involved sealing 486 Davis-Monthan B-29s at $922.66 each; 601 at Pyote, $903.19 each; 55 at San Antonio, $1,019.92 each; and 169 at Oklahoma City, $1,015 each.

175 *History of the AF Storage and Withdrawl Program*, page 48.

176 *Profile History: Military Aircraft Storage and Disposition Center and Predecessor Organizations, 1946–1974*, pp. 4–9.

177 Trester, *History of the AF Storage and Withdrawal Program*, page 26.

178 Ibid, p. 69.

179 Ibid, p. 41.

180 Ibid, p. 45.

181 Ibid, p. 46.

182 Lt. Col. Frank Schirmer. "History of 4105 AAF Base Unit, 1945-1948," *Journal of the American Aviation Historical Society.* AAHS. Spring 1986.

183 Lawrence C. Railing. *Profile History: Military Aircraft Storage and Disposition Center and Predecessor Organizations, 1946–1974*, page 4.

184 Ibid.

185 *Enola Gay* resides at the National Air and Space Museum, Washington, D.C., and the remaining aircraft are at the Air Force Museum, Wright-Patterson AFB, Ohio. Interestingly enough, the B-17 *Swoose*, which was rescued from the smelter at Kingman, and the B-29 *Enola Gay* were flown to the national air museum's storage facility at Park Ridge, Illinois, in 1949. When C-119 production was restarted to support the Korean War, this facility was taken over and the museum aircraft were shipped by ground transportation to Silver Hill, Maryland, scrapped on site, or, in the case of the *Swoose* and *Enola Gay*, flown to Pyote for storage.

186 Trester, *History of the AF Storage and Withdrawl Program, 1945–1952, p. 24.*

187 *Profile History: Military Aircraft Storage and Disposition Center and Predecessor Organizations, 1946–1974*, pp. 4–9.

188 Ibid., p. 11.

189 Ibid., p. 14.

190 Marcelle S. Knaack, *Encyclopedia of U.S. Air Force Aircraft and Missile Systems: Post–World War II Bombers*: Washington, D.C., Office of Air Force History. 1988, p. 490.

191 History of Headquarters, 2704th Air Force Aircraft Storage and Disposition Group, Davis-Monthan AFB, Arizona, 1963.

192 *Encyclopedia of U.S. Air Force Aircraft and Missile Systems*, p. 490.

193 History of Headquarters, 2704th AF Aircraft Storage and Disposition Group, and *MASDC Profile History*, p. 22.

194 *MASDC Profile History*, p. 31.

195 History of Headquarters, 2704th AF Aircraft Storage and Disposition Group, p. 7.

196 Ibid.

197 *Encyclopedia of U.S. Air Force Aircraft and Missile Systems*, p. 154.

198 *MASDC Profile History*, p. 36.

199 *Chronology of Highlights of Aircraft Storage Units.* MASDC.

200 "And Then There Were None!" *Phoenix Gazette*, September 19, 1966.

201 *Chronology of Highlights of Aircraft Storage Units.* MASDC. This included 18 B-66Ds, nine C-47s, 33 T-33s, and 22 Cessna U3Bs.

202 *Encyclopedia of U.S. Air Force Aircraft and Missile Systems* and *Chronology of Highlights of Aircraft Storage Units.*

203 *AMARC: A Diamond in the Desert.* AMARC Business Office.

204 Aircraft destined for museums are supervised by the U.S. Air Force; Headquarters, Air Force Material Command, acts as the liaison for donations to groups other than museums. See Department of the Air Force, *U.S. Air Force Static Display Program: Municipalities and Veterans' Organizations*, AMARC/Air Force Material Command, Davis-Monthan AFB, for a full list of organizational points of contact regarding Army and Navy assets.

INDEX